Architectural Association London
AA Agendas No. 5

TYPOLOGICAL FORMATIONS: RENEWABLE BUILDING TYPES AND THE CITY

Edited by Christopher C. M. Lee & Sam Jacoby
AA Diploma 6

Typological Formations:
Renewable Building Types and the City
Christopher C. M. Lee & Sam Jacoby, AA Diploma 6

AA Agendas Series Editor: Brett Steele
AA Publications Editor: Pamela Johnston
AA Production Editor: Thomas Weaver
AA Art Director: Zak Kyes
Design: Rob Peart
Editorial Assistant: Clare Barrett

AA Publications are produced
through the AA Print Studio.
aaprintstudio.net

Printed in Belgium by Cassochrome

ISBN 978-1-902902-58-6

For a catalogue of AA Publications visit
aaschool.ac.uk/publications
or email publications@aaschool.ac.uk

AA Publications
36 Bedford Square
London WC1B 3ES
T + 44 (0)20 7887 4021
F + 44 (0)20 7414 0783

Contents

SERIAL SENSIBILITIES: A DIAGRAMMATIC FOREWORD TO TYPOLOGICAL FORMATIONS

I.

Typological Formations, edited by Christopher C.M. Lee and Sam Jacoby, asks the following question of architects: does Dubai matter more than the 'diagram'? Asked another way, how are architects supposed to square the rampant commercial and capital forces reshaping cities today with the explosion of information-based design systems that has already, over the past decade, dramatically reconfigured architects' design studios, tools and working methods? It's a smart question, and one that deliberately intertwines the two great challenges facing the generation of architects who are now coming of age: the change being wrought upon the world by entirely new *kinds* of cities being built at unprecedented speeds and scales, and the massive change being brought about in architects' own design studios and work regimes. Whether, or how, these two forms of change could influence one another, and resurrect an architectural design culture understood in relation to the city, is what this book is all about.

This collection of student projects from the AA's Diploma Unit 6 encapsulates a generational shift, not just in how architects view the city, but in architectural knowledge itself. After the past decade of deep (and sometimes, it would appear, deeply self-satisfied) explorations into new digital and computational design tools, *Typological Formations* marks a return to architectural culture. A quick glance through these pages will confirm the obvious: sophisticated parametric tools are all over these projects, but they are no longer a topic or focus in and of themselves. Instead, such tools are merely brought to bear, not only on larger problems or sites, but also – most interestingly – on the late modern terminology and conceptual framework of something like building typology. It's a pretty neat little trick, effectively directing today's most advanced design tools (iterative, scripted design processes) and conceptual orientation (a diagrammatic approach to architectural form) back onto architects' own cultural language.

What makes this collection especially noteworthy in the context of the AA right now is its deep and open commitment to intelligent and comprehensive *design*, specifically *building design*. It's fair to say that the sweeping successes of a 'diagrammatic' turn in experimental architectures around the mid-90s led to building design being largely sidelined in architectural discourse. In schools like the AA, most units and programmes focused on design processes, digital tools, mappings and methodologies, on worlds full of surfaces, structures and components – on anything but buildings. By contrast this modest book points, in a big way, to the productive capacity of *building projects themselves* as a legitimate form of critical architectural knowledge. I read its subtitle, 'Renewable Building Types and the City', as a form of architectural experimentation. A long overdue experiment, it connects the book in another surprising way with the era in which its principal topic, architectural typology, captured architectural imaginations.

II.

In his 1973 *Anxiety of Influence* Harold Bloom writes that it is the job of every artist to first invent (much more than respond to) his or her predecessors. In the case of the work collected in this book, the predecessors are to be found in the 1990s, a period of Aeron Chairs, dot.com stocks and (in architecture) the discourse of the 'diagram'. Let's first recall the long shadows still being cast in the early 90s by post-modern pioneers who had made their mark 20 or 30 years earlier with the publication of travel-book manifestos with names like *Learning from Las Vegas*, *Collage City*, or *Delirious New York*. It was the influence of that generation's view of the city (or perhaps the anxiety engendered by it) that the younger generation of architects absorbed into their 'diagrammatic architectures' work, which first emerged almost exactly a decade ago.

Diagrammatic architectures arrived alongside something else: the most unexpected material transformation that design studios had experienced in nearly a century, with the advent of personal computing and its networked world of peripherals, software and new media. This gave a well-prepared group of young 90s architects a way out of the tired post-modern historicism and deconstructionist hyperbole of the late 80s, allowing them to re-think architecture from the inside out using their own very new design software and machinery, as opposed to history. The 'diagram' and its implicitly networked, informational impetus was the perfect 'concept' for imagining a new kind of architecture in a newly networked, digital world. In an era when, in the famous formulation of Baudrillard, 'simulations' were supposedly more real 'than reality itself', diagrams seemed to fit perfectly.

As the saying goes, timing is everything. The young diagrammers' strategy worked brilliantly: by making their own 'diagrams' and information-based forms of synthesis and design a vital focus of their own work, they seemed to have found a convincing means for *really* (finally) leaving Las Vegas, Manhattan and Rome behind. But a few years ago, something strange happened to upset the smooth surface of contemporary diagrammatic architectures: architects of all kinds started getting very busy, cities started mattering again as the world started building, or re-building, more of them than ever before. This is where Chris and Sam's work gets interesting, in that they choose the rapidly changing circumstances of cities in an era of global capitalism as the overt site not just for their architecture, but for their architectural thinking.

III.
Sometime during the past few years, and in ways that are an aggregate consequence of countless seismic shifts in the operations of global capital and development, architects began to wake up to the changed realities driving the greatest wave of construction and building ever confronted by the modern profession, itself now largely globalised in its formation. The assumed epistemological legitimacy of parametric or computational approaches to design, initially aligned simply with the arrival of late-twentieth-century digital life, was overshadowed by an even more pressing professional change: a massive global upswing, at an unprecedented scale and speed, in new building and urban development.

IV.
Chris and Sam were a couple of brave young architects when, three years ago, they decided to launch a new AA Diploma School unit focusing on urbanism as a *design agenda* (rather than on the advanced digital and parametric tools which their students were nonetheless fluent in and wedded to). Their search for 'renewable' building types able to negotiate the realities reconfiguring twenty-first-century cities has already yielded some incredible early results, as this book attests. *Typological Formations* is, I suspect, nothing less than a manifesto for a return to projects and *project-based* forms of architectural knowledge today. This is the field that has really been opened up by an overt return to the presumed architectural 'culture' of building types, as seen through the iterative and serial sensibility of advanced parametric and computational approaches to design. It's a breakthrough, and the book speaks coherently in both retroactive as well as proactive ways – to its recent (diagrammatic) predecessors as well as to the equally optimistic (future) fellow students and travellers who will take this work forward. With this book the idea of an architectural 'type' seems more supple – that is, more differentiated and therefore more relevant and productive – than ever. Judge for yourself, in the many types that follow.

Brett Steele
London, August 2007

5

AA Diploma 6
Students 2004–2007

Mei Mei Chan

Elfreda Chan

Shin Hyung Cho

Deena Fakhro

Catharina Frankander

Marco Ginex

Sheau-Fei Hoe

Suk-Kyu Hong

Martin Jameson

Ruth Kedar

Minseok Kim

Sang-Yun Kim

Keisuke Kobayashi

Florence Kong

Benjamin Koren

Bolam Lee

Keong Wee Lim

Chih-Da Lin

Nankuei Lin

Dan Narita

Yicheng Pan

Charles Peronnin

Rachel Scarr-Hall

Bart Schoonderbeek

Erez Shani

Harold Tan

Christopher Thorn

Valeria Segovia Trigueros

Kelvin Chu Ka Wing

Max von Werz

Hong Chieh Yow

Freda Yuen

INTRODUCTION

Sam and I are from the generation of students who witnessed the moment when parametric digital experimentation first took hold, the generation that began our architectural education with a more critical slant, with the city as our playground, and ended our studies discovering, in cautious awe, the generative power of digital tools.

When we returned to the AA as unit masters in 2002, the sophistication of this trajectory of digital research was altogether evident, in a general shift towards a highly articulated, small-scale formal research driven largely by the prowess of modelling or scripting softwares. This shift also entailed a conscious retreat from investigations of urbanism and, to a certain extent, from the question of architecture's potential in the city. Yet we had witnessed at first hand the relentless growth of cities in China and India, and had come back to London to find a revitalised regeneration climate. We wanted to understand these new conditions better – to find ways of re-engaging with the city.

We began with the simple observation that the dominant material manifestations of the city are building types. Types are prolific in urban plans and have been used by many different generations of architects to shape the city. This focus, we believed, would agitate the stable conception of type, leading us to understand it as renewable, as the pliant and contingent elemental part of the urban plan.

This book documents the three-year investigation of our unit, focusing on the relevance of a renewed interest in typology as a tool for reasoning and producing the urban plan. The conditions and themes that framed our students' work are outlined in the unit briefs (part summary, part contingent manifesto), which are reproduced on the following pages. The projects themselves are divided into two parts, in accordance with their approach to the question of type and the urban plan. *Figuring* contains projects that deal with the possibility of cultivating renewable types from the conditions of the site. Conversely, *Grounding* brings together projects that begin with a dominant type and then, through the differentiation of type's deep structure, transfer its performance onto the ground of the site in order to shape the urban plan.

This book would not have been possible without the support of Brett Steele, Director of the Architectural Association. He not only showed sustained interest in our work, but also helped us to focus and refine the trajectory of our questions and struggles.

The students of AA Diploma Unit 6 have participated in this journey into the unknown, sometimes equipped only with half-drawn maps. We wish to express our gratitude to them all for their contributions, energy, inventiveness and dramas.

Our heartfelt thanks to Lawrence Barth, who is very much part of AA Dip 6, for his intellectual generosity and efforts. Our special thanks also to Hanif Kara for his continued support and help in our search for the generative logic of structural investigations. Our gratitude also goes to Michael Weinstock for his guidance and constant support.

Many thanks to Kelvin Chu Ka Wing, Yicheng Pan, Yael Gilad and Hun-min Kim for their efforts and skills in directing the unit's design workshops.

Last, but not least, our thanks to Mohsen Mostafavi for giving us our first break.

Christopher C.M. Lee and Sam Jacoby

UNIT BRIEFS 2004–2007

2004/05:
Programmatic Afterlives: LONDON 2013

Performative Anomalies

Spurred on by the predicaments of reconciling practice and research, we posit our understanding of architecture as primarily a material practice based on strategic mediation and opportunistic negotiation. While architecture is intrinsically and productively linked to a theoretical framework and self-referential systems, it inevitably operates outside its own internal discourse, being affected by economic, cultural and political forces.

Continuing this interest in contaminated processes, and expanding on previous research on structure/texture, we will be investigating the relationship between structure and programme. The focus for this investigation is the abstraction and propagation of renewable types, eventually leading to mutation and adaptation to difficult and contentious programmatic conditions.

We will begin by looking at structure's potential to create volumetric effects: volumes that induce occupation and events, that seed programmatic conditions with their corresponding sensation. Conversely, the demand of programme stretches the volumetric envelope to engender new conceptions of structure. This mutual agitation reinforces the fitness of the type in question, making it both efficacious and pleasurable.

London 2013

2,900 days of planning and construction. £4.9 billion of public funds. 16 days of delirious use. Then what?

The vision for the London 2012 bid for the Olympics goes far beyond the promotion of the city as the unchallenged cultural hub of Europe, a position it has already secured. London 2012 will bring together a wide range of political and institutional organisations with agendas to promote tourism and business as well as foster lasting urban regeneration, on a national scale. The epicentre of this Herculean task is one of the most deprived regions of the country, the Lea Valley, a 600-hectare green-field area stretching from Hackney Marches down to the River Thames. If London's bid is successful, this valley will be the site of a 200-hectare Olympic Park.

We will begin with an analysis of the proposed strategic masterplan for London 2012, with a bias towards the post-Olympics impact, investigating political and economic agendas versus urban renewal and long-term development needs. The derelict edges of the proposed Olympic Park will be our primary focus.

We will assess the value of iconic planning as a promotional tool and develop alternative planning and building strategies that will both enable the hosting of the Games and provide multiple after-lives for the whole Olympic development.

The primary scale of operation will be that of a building. We will focus on the issues of mobility, growth, organisation, building types and programme to engender an adaptability of renewable types.

Through this we will reconsider the meaning of landmarks and propose a series of alternative buildings or structures, envisioned for impact in 2012 but articulated for resonance beyond 2013.

2005/06:
Programmatic Afterlives 2: LANDMARKS

If urbanity is the composite effect of dominant types, research into the nature and potential of twenty-first century types is critical in any attempt to stage alternative visions for our cities today.

AA Dip 6 will continue to investigate the generative nature of renewable types and their eventual adaptation to contentious urban situations. This line of enquiry requires the positioning of architecture as primarily a material practice based on strategic mediation and opportunism. While theoretical research can be productively pursued as part of an internal discourse, architecture's techniques and insights gain their potency once they are agitated by external forces, subjected to economic, cultural, environmental and political pressures.

Thus the methods we employ are both strategic and tactical, straddling two extreme scales, requiring critical enquiry into the overarching conditions of urbanism and the deployment of generative systemic techniques in specific sites.

Grand Designs Revisited

The Angel of the North. The Shard of Glass. The Gherkin. What constitutes the redemptive power of these landmarks, or their allure for the public, is largely contentious. Contemporary cities increasingly define themselves through the spectacle of their architecture and icons, from Shanghai to Dubai, and now London. Propelled by market economies, these major new urban developments seek aggrandisement through the proliferation of landmark structures. The resulting escalation of strategic differentiation in a climate of perpetual promotional panic has created a new breed of landmark-types, seemingly indispensable until the inevitable introduction of the next rival landmark.

The impending London Olympics has exacerbated this condition, though it has also triggered a wave of optimistic grand speculations. Over the next 20 years the city will undergo structural changes of a magnitude unknown since 1666. London's historical domestic scale will be challenged, its density significantly increased, its metropolitan borders breached and its persistent resistance to absolutist planning severely put to the test.

We will begin by revisiting the breeding ground of these landmark-types and masterplans, from White City to Stratford City. We will reassess the validity of hinging the success of an urban plan on landmarks and propose alternative visions for London through a series of buildings and structures that seek to elude their own expiry while aspiring to provide sustenance for an urbanity that resonates beyond the immediate demands of market economies.

2006/07:
Renewable Types: LEISURE CITIES

At the heart of AA Dip 6's investigation is a rethinking of the effect of types beyond their immediate singular and architectural scale, whereby types are understood as a collective urban entity that holds the potential to seed, differentiate, regulate and administer the urban plan.

Going beyond the paradoxical freedom of employing traditional precedents as a starting point and reaching new solutions through the subsequent formal variation of types, we propose to position typological reasoning between the generation of new and independently emergent types and the regulation of adaptive and opportunistic urban plans through the mutual differentiation and adaptation of the deep structures of both types and the city.

To rethink and thus re-envision dominant types inevitably raises questions of control, flexibility, difference and participation – and most acutely the need to address the issue of programmatic after-lives, the ability of the type to renew or reconfigure itself over time to elude eventual expiry. We will expand this cross-scalar investigation by considering the potential of type to affect issues of economic, social and environmental renewal, staged through a reactive pliant urban plan.

Learning from Las Vegas Redux

Urban regeneration fuelled by the promiscuous union of leisure, tourist and gaming industries has spawned a whole new generation of worldwide leisure cities, driven by types for distractions and amusement. These types range from the gladiatorial colosseums and bath complexes of ancient times to the theme parks, museums and supercasinos of the present day.

Spearheading this international development is Singapore's £1.7 billion Integrated Resort, a euphemism for what will be the largest casino in Asia, hot on the heels of Macau's 650-hectare Cotai Strip. At the same time, a total of 68 local authorities in the UK, including Blackpool, Wembley Stadium, Cardiff, Glasgow, the Millennium Dome, Manchester, Newcastle upon Tyne and Sheffield have hedged their bets on the potential of supercasinos to regenerate their cities and boroughs: Las Vegas Style.

The proliferation of a dominant type is an increasingly common strategy for reinventing cities – think of the Olympics and their telegenic stadiums, the defunct industrial towns and their artertainment museums, and now the defunct themed cities and their supercasinos. The dominant type seemingly offers the required conflated image of spectacle, singular vision, confidence through scale and critical mass all in one deft gesture.

Transplanting these omnipresent leisure types into cities represents a kind of Faustian pact: the promise of vast revenues for urban regeneration in exchange for the city hosting a benign tumour. Neither dismissing the supercasino from the very outset nor accepting it in its current form, we will re-examine these aspiring cities, boroughs and their proposals, to investigate and re-imagine the role of renewable dominant types and alternative sustainable visions for our cities.

Leisure cities today are too ubiquitous to be relegated to the status of urbanism's trivia.

1.0
FIGURING

Yicheng Pan, Resisting the Generic Empire

1.1
PERFORATED HILL

Kelvin Chu Ka Wing

Site: Lea Valley / Stratford, London

The Olympic Legacy Plan promises future regeneration for London yet requires the demolition and reconstruction of more than 50 per cent of the infrastructure and structures built for the 2012 games. This project invents an alternative strategy. Instead of using individual forms such as the stadium to organise the Olympic park, it proposes collective forms that establish nodal development sites for a polycentric network within the Lea Valley.

This strategy directly reworks the typology of the stadium, the largest contributor to the redundancy of the games. It transforms its compact organisation into a perforated and dispersed model with an integrated transport node below the pitch. It also looks at how the stadiums can provide programmed and occupied bridges to span the railways and roads that currently cut off the Lea Valley from its surroundings.

The resultant urban fabric seamlessly combines transport nodes, open spaces and built volumes, using circulatory branching models to meet the stadiums' requirements for crowd dispersal and holding. By exploiting the layered growth of branching, these structures generate a three-dimensional circulation pattern (as distinct from traditional, horizontal two-dimensional grids). A new multi-layered vertical system of ownership and programme distribution accommodates diverse user groups and programmes at different phases in the development, without the need for large-scale demolition.

Bifurcations of the circulation systems occur both horizontally and vertically. The vertical bifurcation separates user groups and establishes separate security zones for athletes and visitors. During the Olympics, visitors occupy the top and bottom levels, whilst the sandwiched layers in between accommodate local programmes such as offices, retail and housing, which receive sunlight through the voids created by the horizontal bifurcation. In contrast to a conventional grid, with its vertical stacking, the vertical bifurcation also provides a greater level of flexibility, weaving together continuous programmatic layers in tandem with the functional switches of the masterplan.

Where all the layers and bifurcated routes come together, the stadium pitch and the transport nodes create spaces organised in the same way as popular landmarks like Piccadilly Circus. These act as urban mega-nodes within the Lea Valley, consolidating local network and infrastructural links while encouraging communication between the segregated boroughs.

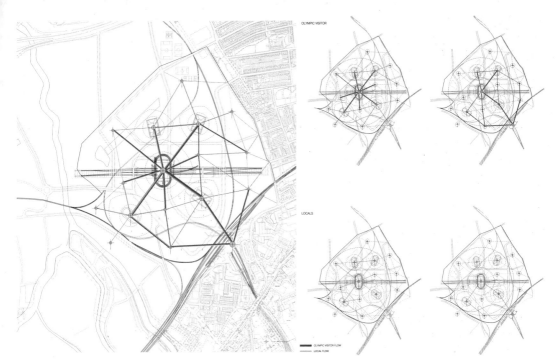

Polycentric network organisation

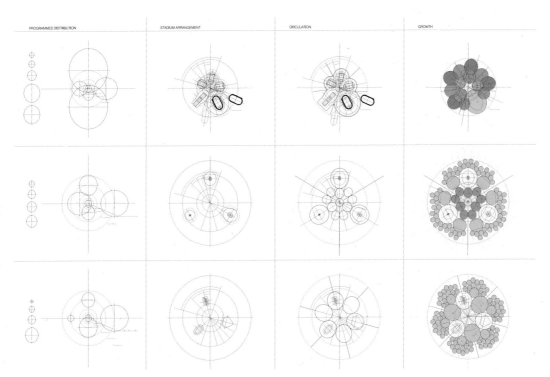

Nodal hierachies

The strategic aim of the masterplan is to locate intensive nodes – stadiums clustered with infrastructural hubs – that will act as new growth centres, linking into the existing polycentric network between Stratford City, Hackney Wick and Pudding Mill Lane.

15

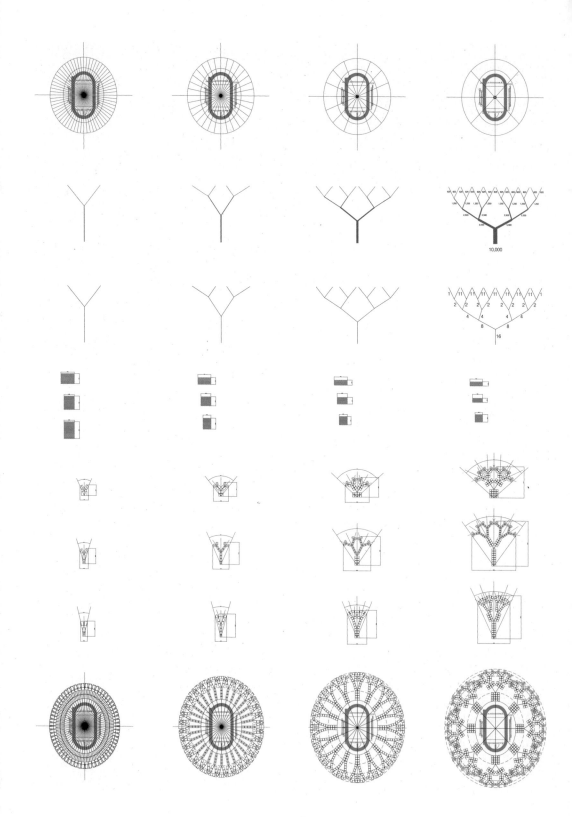

Accessing the stadium from below – rather than from its edges – allows the local circulation pattern to be consolidated underneath the pitch. The lower concourse functions as a holding area to absorb crowds, thus allowing the clustering and variation of the stadium typology.

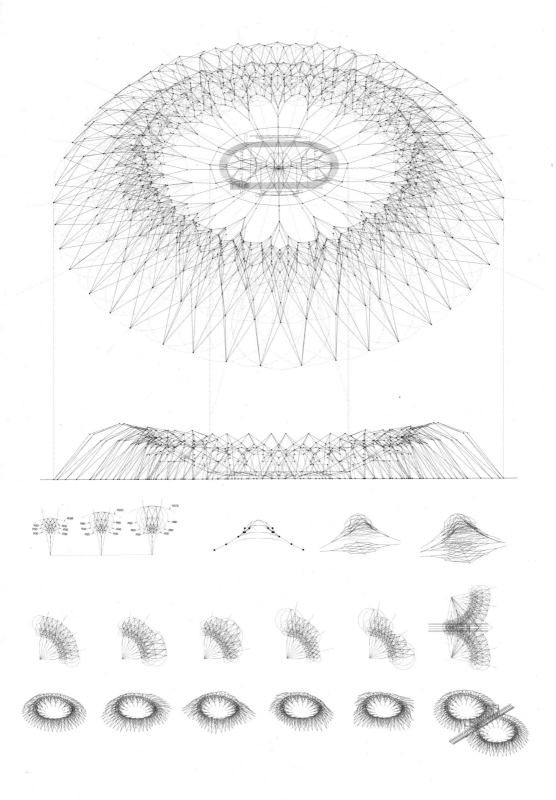

A study of different structural systems – from column branches to cantilevers, catenaries and arches – points to means of achieving several distinct edge conditions leading to the bridging and clustering of stadiums.

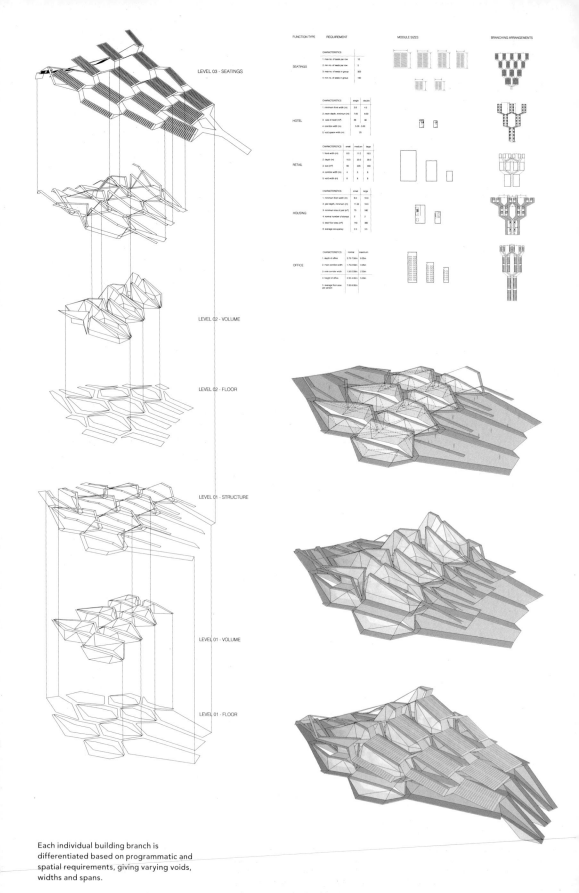

Each individual building branch is
differentiated based on programmatic and
spatial requirements, giving varying voids,
widths and spans.

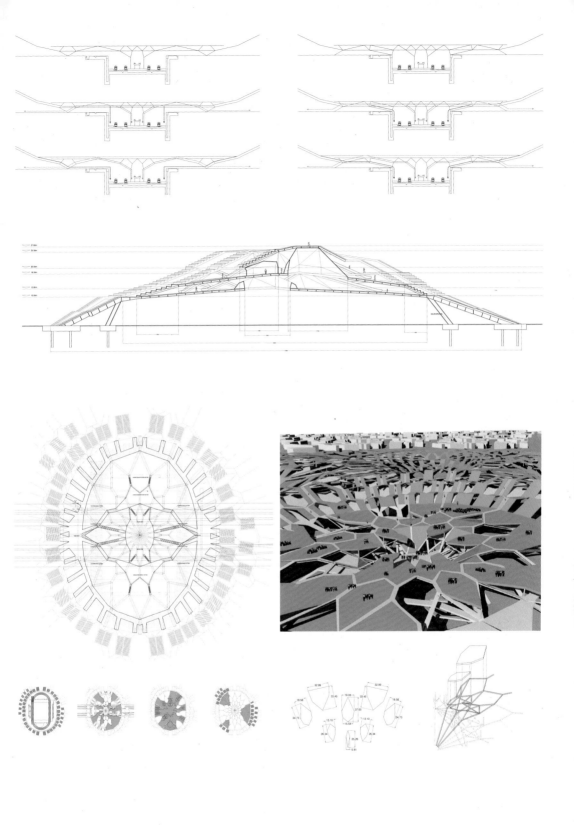

Each structural layer of the truss-arch skeleton provides for different programme types and voids, whereby the spatial and volumetric density and size relate to the overall flow capacity.

The structure is formed of prefabricated joint modules, stabilised by concrete panels poured on site. The pitch is composed of a series of regular panels. After the Olympics, some of these can be removed to allow the pitch to be converted into a number of smaller public spaces, while opening up the concourse level below.

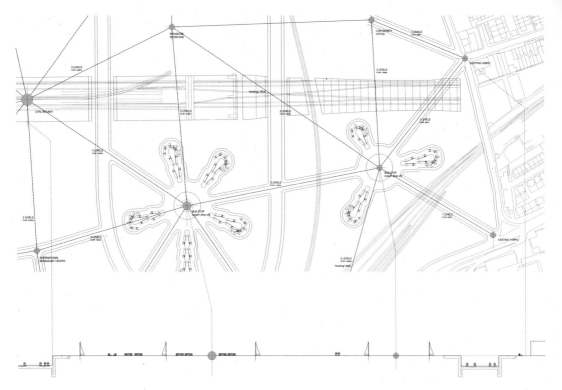

2005–06: Infrastructure preparation
Work during this stage focuses on preparing the ground condition, including the road and railway. The foundation of the arch structure is put in place, as is the bus station under the stadium.

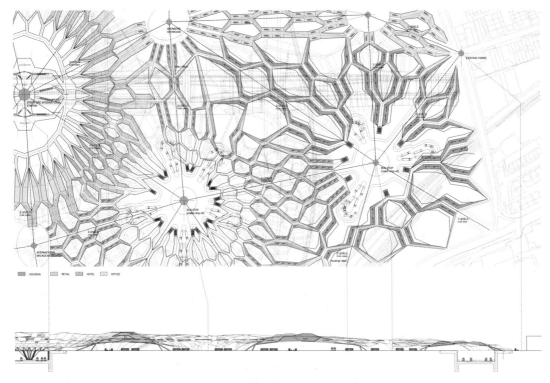

2007–11: Pre-Olympic phase
The middle layers of the arch structure are constructed and populated with housing, hotels, offices and retail. The branching structures converge into transport nodes forming the train station and completing the bus station.

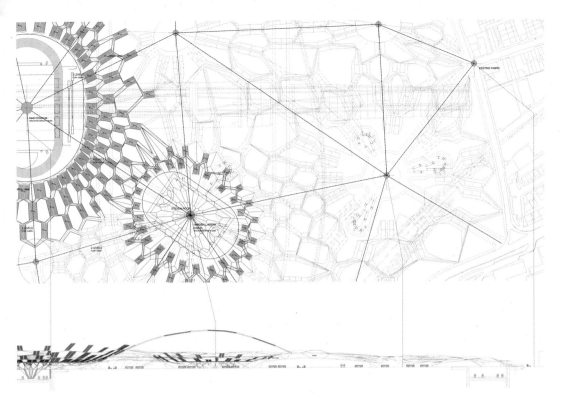

2012: Olympic phase
Installation of the top layer of the structure, including the roof of the indoor stadium and the temporary seating. The pitch over the rail station concourse and bus station is also built.

2013: Post-Olympic park
After the games the seating and some of the panels that make up the pitch are removed. The pitch is then merged with the transport nodes into a public space, while the top layer is converted into a continuous roof garden and amenity space for the programmes below.

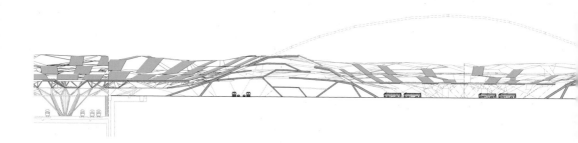

Typical section, plan and elevation of the main stadium cluster, which forms a programmatic and structural perforated hill functioning both as sports structure and public park with integrated transport hub and concourse. By bridging disruptive physical barriers, the resultant fabric forms seamless connections between transport nodes, open spaces and building volumes, which are constructed as autonomous layers that accommodate the varying requirements during the programmatic switches of the different masterplan phases.

Olympics-driven urbanism has always been burdened with the inevitable redundancy of large-scale sport facilities within desolate areas that lack infrastructural connections or a resident population. Rather than trying to convert obsolete structures into a functioning city after the game, this project proposes a new and connected neighbourhood within a larger existing polycentric network that is capable of absorbing the short-term Olympic event.

1.2
INTERIORISED URBANISM
Valeria Segovia Trigueros

Site: Battersea Power Station, London

There have been many attempts in the past to redevelop Sir Giles Gilbert Scott's power station in Battersea. All have failed because of their inability to address the problems of the scale of the power station and its isolation within the residual post-industrial fabric of southwest London. The solution proposed here is to compress and consolidate programmes for the site within a united type – the Megatype.

Of a similar scale to the derelict power station, this Megatype avoids the predicament of conversion and preserves the building's iconic status while removing or bridging the existing physical obstacles to redevelopment, in particular the railway viaduct to the west. In parallel, by merging structure, services and circulation, it allows for the differentiation of void-to-programme ratios and the coexistence of dissimilar programmes within a compact footprint, so freeing up the ground for future development.

In projecting the structural growth of the Megatype, two models are explored – the Voronoi and branching patterns. The resulting distribution method creates a maximum flexibility within this 'interiorised urban' type and a high level of control over the dispersal of key public passages. Future growth and programmatic seeding are controlled by the strategic positioning of the arterial structural system, with its implied void-to-solid relationship. The final capacity matches that of the current masterplan by Parkview.

As the Megatype facilitates incremental growth and does not depend on the completion of the masterplan quota, the site can be completed in response to funding and changing programmatic needs. The initial phases insert the primary structural arteries or infrastructural passages that establish new points of access to the site from the west and create an extension to Battersea Park, while simultaneously acting as the superstructure of the future Megatype. Subsequent phases provide for the inhabitation of the Megatype by first installing public recreational programmes within the superstructure and then slowly filling the voids with volumes and secondary infrastructure/structures for the required programmes.

As the Megatype is regulated through the distribution of its voids, planar and sectional differentiation within the fabric of the block is still possible during each phase, though the final growth and density is controlled to guarantee a functional public realm throughout.

The organisation of voids changes depending on the angle, length, number and location of growth points of a particular branch type. Here, a central and a peripheral branching system is tested within a volume equivalent in size to Battersea Power Station.

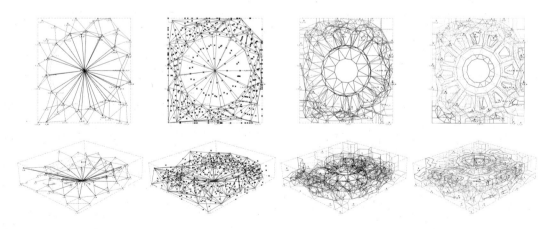

The use of the Voronoi diagram allows the decomposition of a metric space determined by distances to a specified discrete set of points, vertices or volumes. The space of the Megatype is subdivided by points distributed to derive its area of influence and three-dimensional voids.

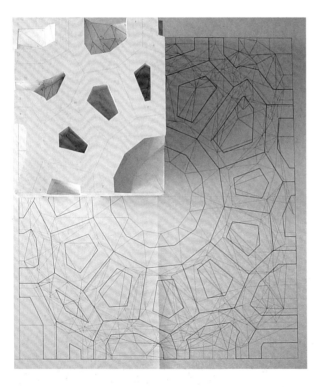

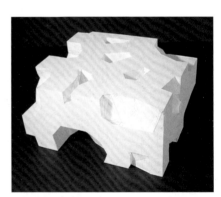

Voronoi model

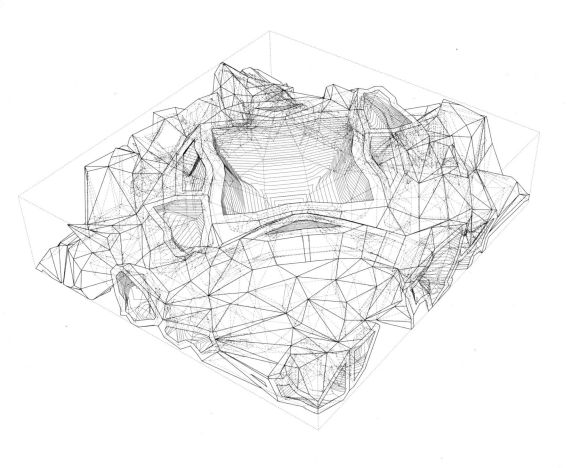

Branching model

The performance of the generic branching and Voronoi models is compared, and as branching produces more hierarchy and compactness it is developed further. Its structure approaches an arch, allowing the bridging of the surrounding railway arches and access from Battersea Park.

Furthermore, the courtyard-like organisation gives a clear hierarchy of structure and circulation, enabling the controlled distribution of routes and programmes through the distribution of the fixed void-to-solid ratios which are required by the different functions.

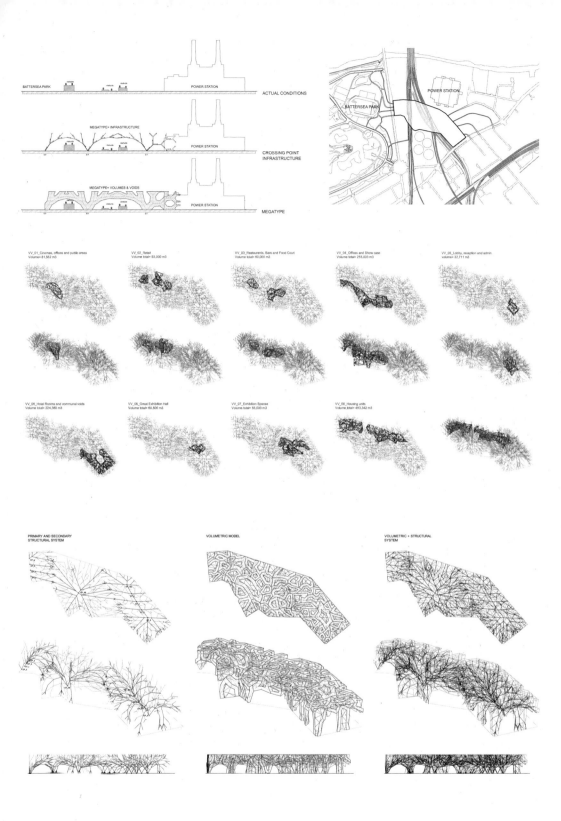

The proposed Megatype consolidates the required amount of programme through the organisation and distribution of interior voids, thus producing an interiorised urbanism. Whilst the Power Station remains untouched, its landmark status is intensified through juxtaposition of scale, and access to the formerly segregated site is improved by linking it to Battersea Park.

The Megastructure is constructed incrementally. The first thing to be implemented is the infrastructure and the primary structure, a bi-directional arch that provides both the superstructure and the circulation space. Then the secondary structure, with its programmatic volumes, is locally inserted as required. The volumetric completion is anticipated to match that of the current masterplan and is controlled by the structural and programmatic distribution of void-to-solid ratios.

Incremental growth

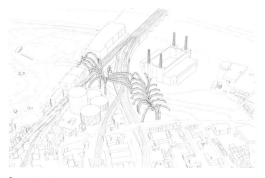

Superstructure

Secondary structure

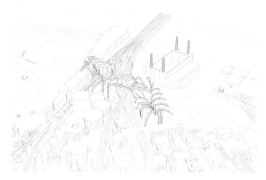

Entertainment volumes

Hotel volumes

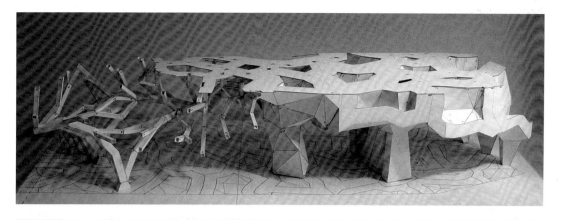

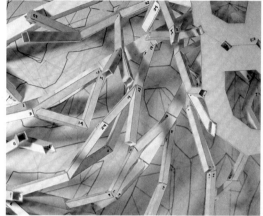

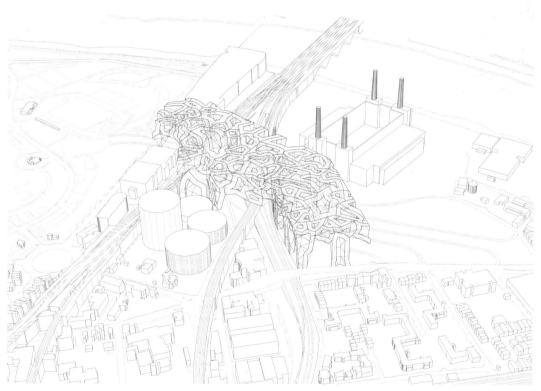

Volumetric completion

1.3
MEDIATED SPECTACLE
Keisuke Kobayashi

Site: Central London

The success of the Olympics is increasingly tied to the role played by the media: in 2012 an anticipated two billion people will experience the games via their television screens, 600 times the number of actual visitors.

The preoccupation with spectacle is reflected in the London 2012 Marathon route, which loops three times around the city centre, highlighting London's iconic buildings as a televisual backdrop.

Taking advantage of this phenomenon, the strategy of this proposal is to graft the Olympic events directly onto media-intense sites within central London, while at the same time extending the marathon route to the Lea Valley to take in run-down areas of east London. Distributed along the route are new Olympic landmarks that can later be converted into housing, forming the beginnings of regeneration through association. Through their association with the Olympic spectacle and the provision of new infrastructure and housing, the value of these areas is immediately increased.

In the centre of London a prominent site by the London Eye is redesignated an 'Olympic village'. A series of floating linear structures are deployed along the river, in vertical stacks. During the day they form amphitheatres for sporting events, while at night they are transformed into open spaces for athletes.

The housing structures are based on a combination of six basic lightweight frame modules. The stacking of the prefabricated individual units and the multiple strands of adjacent chains creates different levels of setback and open spaces, allowing varied volumetric occupation and programmatic possibilities. The interlocking of the units also provides the necessary structural stiffness. After the games, the structures are floated downriver, to serve as permanent housing within the ambitious Thames Gateway development.

The over-provision of open spaces within the chain structure allows for greater variety in the housing types and for adaptation to future needs. The value of the housing units is heightened by their direct role in the Olympic event as well as by their own iconography.

The Marathon route is extended from iconic
central London to derelict parts of Hackney:
regeneration through association.

Erection of modular housing units to serve as
Olympic village and sports structure during
the games.

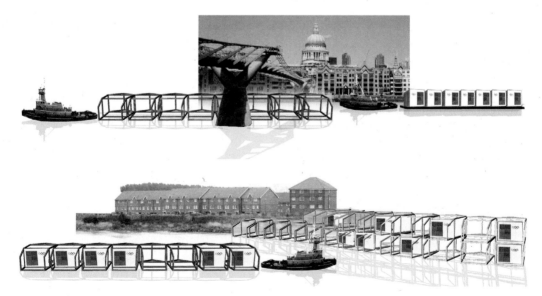

After the games, the chains are floated
downriver to serve as permanent housing units
in the Thames Gateway.

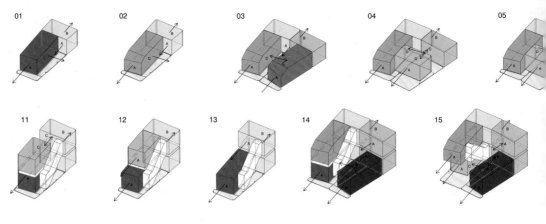

Modular housing components

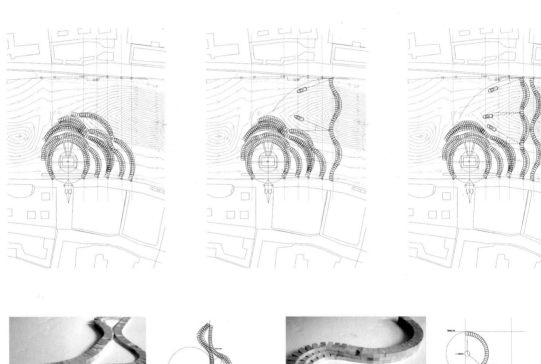

Chain studies

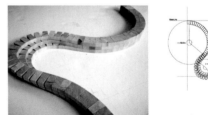

Transformation sequence

The aim of the new masterplan based on the marathon route is to place temporary structures near established landmark sites to intensify the mediated spectacle.

For the river sites, modular units – consisting of six prefabricated modules in 20 combinations – serve as temporary sports structures during the day and as athlete accommodation at night. The chain-linked structures are retractable and dynamic in order to enable these opposed functions. When no sporting event is taking place, the chains act as a public structure that links the south and north banks of the river, intensifying the connections between existing landmarks.

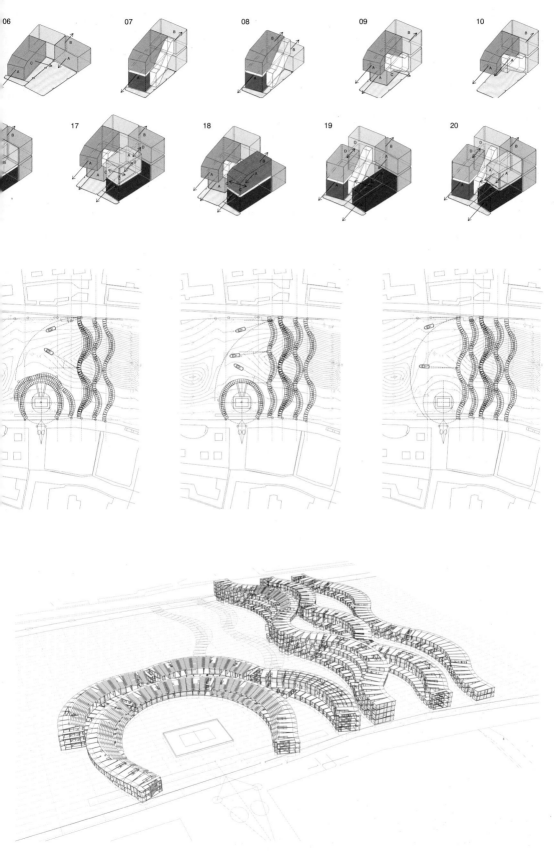

Typical configuration during the games

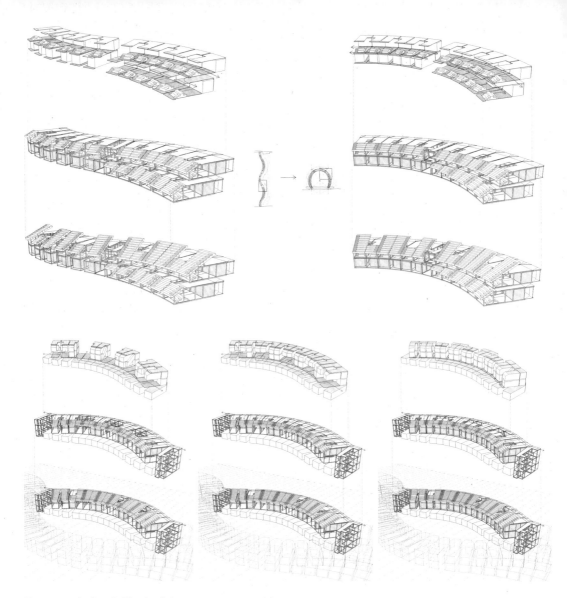

Fragment study of a typical floating chain
segment, looking at the performative and
structural changes required to enable the
varying configurations of the chain modules,
from stadium with seating to bridge with
public access and high-security athlete
housing with private zones.

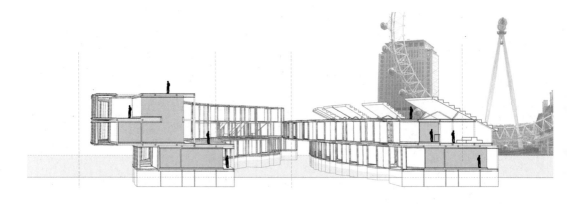

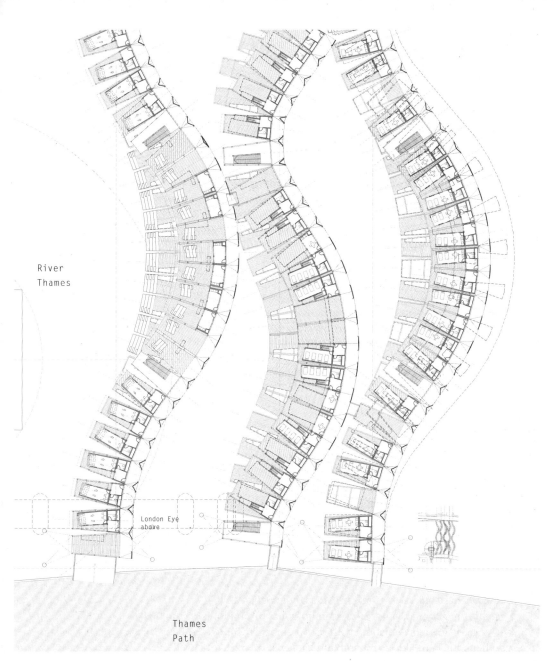

River
Thames

London Eye
above

Thames
Path

Part plan at London Eye

1.4
PERIPHERAL TYPOLOGY

Yicheng Pan

Site: Lea Valley, London

Sudden demographic changes in the wake of the industrial revolution transformed London into a sprawling metropolis. More than 150 years later, planners are still contesting the actual location of the city's shifting centre and the erratic urban sprawl continues in defiance of the mechanisms that were devised to contain it: the ring roads, which radiate out from inner London to the periphery, and the encircling green belt, which imposes an abrupt break in density, signifying the outer limits of the city.

The Lower Lea Valley is a unique site that demonstrates a combination of these two mechanisms, being part of a green belt situated outside the inner ring road of London. Set up as a bastion against unmediated urban expansion, it was quickly infiltrated, encroached on and eventually abandoned. The ring road, as a largely utilitarian piece of infrastructure, lacks the organisational capacity to manage urban sprawl. Instead it has exacerbated the condition of the edge, its array of self-referential orientations and alignments giving rise to unconsolidated and residual spaces. The adjoining parkland, too, has fallen victim to inconsistent policies on its preservation. It has succumbed to the relentless march of industrialisation, becoming a dumping-ground for urban misfits – huge box-like factories and warehouses. Together, these two effects have created a city-edge phenomenon, lacking the necessary nodalities and avenues for a centralised plan.

The 2012 Olympics, with its impetus for large-scale construction, offers the perfect opportunity to redefine this edge, reinstate lost parkland and regenerate the area as a whole. This project attempts to reconcile city edge and lost parkland by concentrating and densifying the Olympic structures into a coherent and programmatically intensified urban edge with a clear demarcation of growth. The traditionally concentric stadium typology is restructured as a linear development that can be organised as a series of fused nodes, with the resulting lop-sided typology responding to spectator distribution, circulation and safety zone requirements.

To create a coherent whole, the broken programmatic lines along the Lea Valley are extended into the new volumes of the linear development. The stadiums adapt to the various existing edge conditions either by opening their voids to the surrounding fabric to consolidate residual spaces, or by merging with the parkland.

During the Olympics, when there is a strict segregation of use, the spectators can freely inhabit the public parkland while the intensified edge is occupied by athletes and support staff. Afterwards the Legacy Plan dissolves this segregation. Strips of programmes (i.e., housing, retail, offices) are inserted and extended from the existing fabric, thickening and bulging around the nodes and forming a newly revitalised city edge.

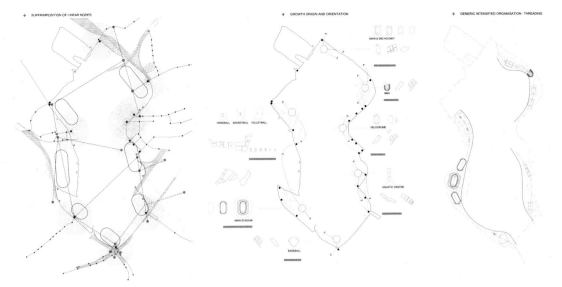

Linear nodes along the Lea Valley periphery are identified as sites that require either the consolidation of residual land – the connecting of broken programmatic lines within the surrounding city fabric – or the clear demarcation of growth to protect the internal parkland. These linear nodes are structurally dependent on the placement of Olympic facilities.

Locally, the concentric stadium typology is transformed into a lop-sided organisation that allows for the articulation of internal or external intensified edge conditions.

A series of contextual transformations of the stadium type occur through a connecting of broken physical and programmatic lineages.

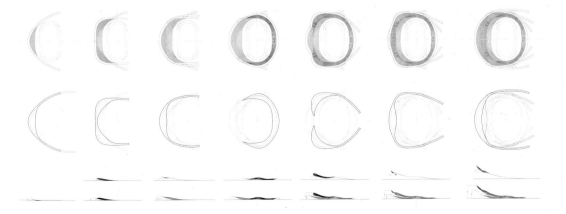

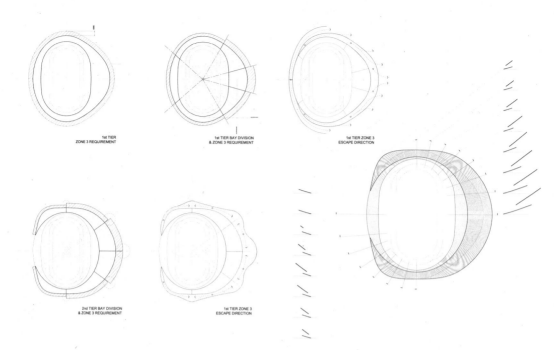

1st TIER
ZONE 3 REQUIREMENT

1st TIER BAY DIVISION
& ZONE 3 REQUIREMENT

1st TIER ZONE 3
ESCAPE DIRECTION

2nd TIER BAY DIVISION
& ZONE 3 REQUIREMENT

1st TIER ZONE 3
ESCAPE DIRECTION

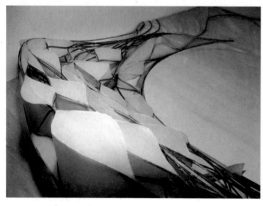

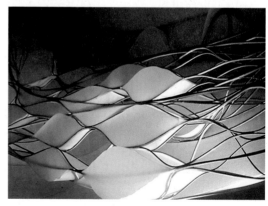

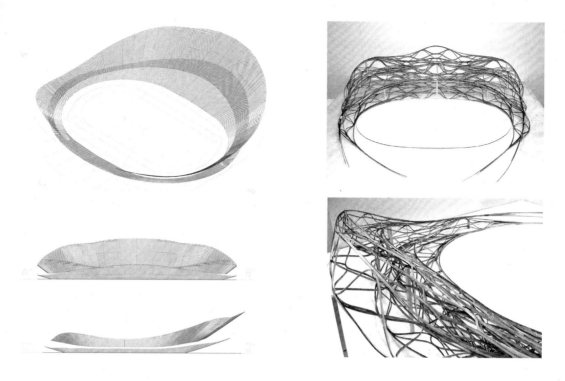

Main stadium model

The typological differentiation of the stadium is regulated through the safety zone and escape route planning, but also takes into account viewing angles and seating capacity. This then generates a generic structure in which the specific contextual programmatic and infrastructural strands from the city fabric are woven into and lead to the inhabitation of the primary structure by programme volumes and seating platforms.

The masterplan is regulated by a series of either bundled or woven programmatic strips that provide for housing, retail, commercial, or infrastructural (loop roads) and pedestrian circulation. These are informed by the city periphery or the parkland, as well as by the requirements for security and safety zones. After the Olympics, stadiums are either converted into public spaces or integrated into the parkland.

Infrastructure and green pedestrian strips

White sites

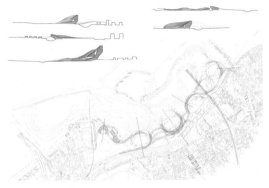

Retail strips

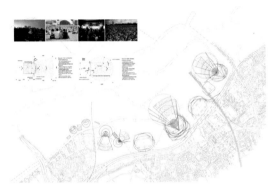

Post-Olympic event spaces

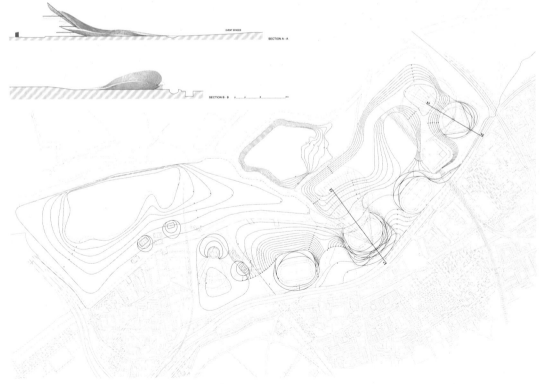

Ground modification

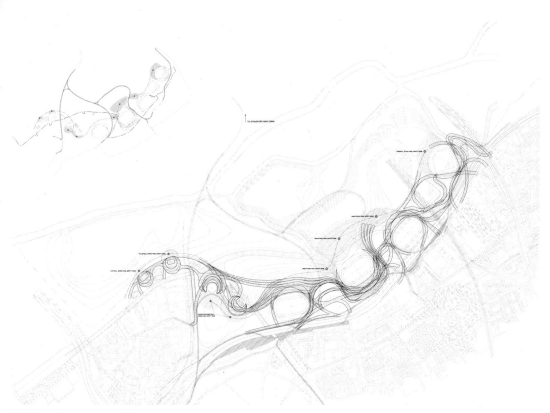

2012 Olympics spectator circulation

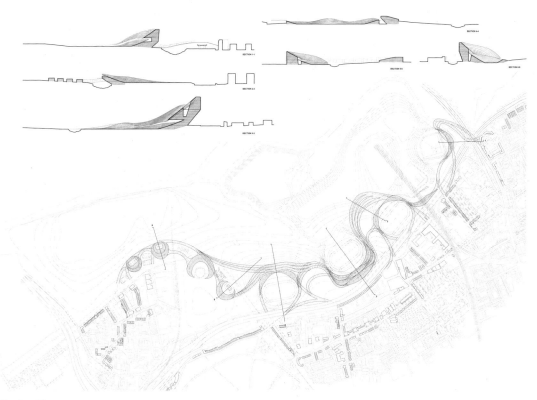

Housing strips

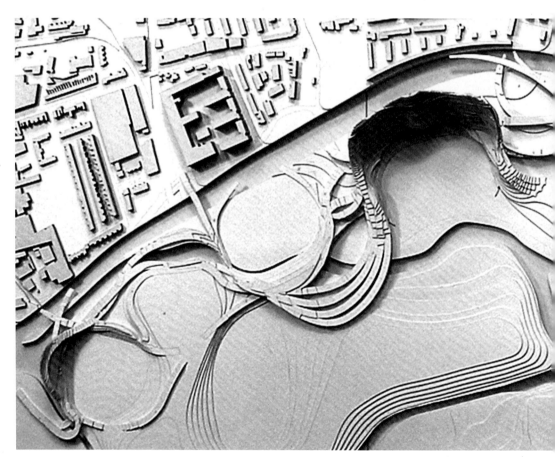

Masterplan model

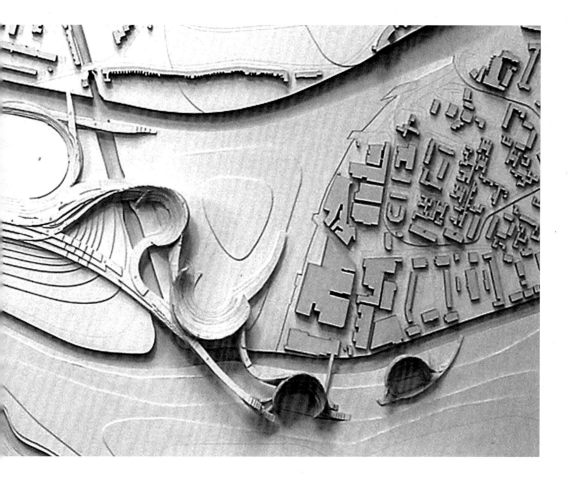

1.5
THE PROJECTIVE ARCADE
Max von Werz

Site: White City, London

The Arcade Type Reconsidered

The arcade as a building type emerged in the nineteenth century, marking a shift from a culture of production to one of consumption. In Paris alone more than 300 arcades offered an alternative universe, parallel to the visible world of streets, where consumers or *flâneurs* could stroll aimlessly in a seductive dream state, famously described by Walter Benjamin in his arcades project as 'phantasmagoria'. The proposal projects this abandoned building type into our contemporary urban situation as a connective structure, suggesting an open shopping type that is beneficial to the social and urban fabrics of the city. Thus, the 'arcades project' becomes the 'Projective Arcade'.

The Projective Arcade

The Projective Arcade is a critique of the extreme mono-functionality and enclosure of the generic shopping mall, which ignores shopping's potential to seed urban regeneration (as the last remaining form of 'public activity') and literally turns its back on the city. One excessive instance of this interiorised and disconnected type is currently being developed in White City, west London, at a cost of £1.6 billion – Westfield's mall, a big box that will be the largest shopping centre in Europe, boasting 15 hectares of retail flooring.

As an alternative scenario, this project proposes to disperse the planned shopping centre and its commercial programmes around the periphery of the W12 masterplan by OMA. In place of a box-like mall, a highly localised and inclusive arcade structure consolidates conflicting edge conditions and reactivates desolate, long-neglected strips of redundant spaces and programmes.

This new model conceives a generic arcade type as an urban infrastructure running along the periphery of the site. By increasing the perpendicular permeability and introducing a set of lateral stretched arches, the arcade becomes a structural framework which ties into and consolidates disparate fabrics, overcoming the local segregation caused by the existing large-scale transportation infrastructure. The proposal advocates phasing in the form of cumulative programmatic layers which themselves seek to challenge the flatness of shopping types and the conventions of the two-dimensional urban plan, resulting in a three-dimensional urban design guideline reorganising the edges. In the words of architectural historian J.F. Geist, the arcade should be 'seen not only as a historical object but also as a contemporary possibility'.

A) INTERFACES
- 1 Shinfield St Housing
- 2 Wood Lane Car Park
- 3 Bulwer St Housing
- 4 Latimer Industrial Estate
- 5 Wood Lane Retail Strip
- 6 Wood Lane Housing 1
- 7 Wood Lane Housing 2

B) SLIVERS
- 1 Westway Flyover (west)
- 2 Westway Flyover (site)
- 3 Hammersmith Line Viaduct
- 4 Westway Sports Centre

C) ISLANDS
- 1 West Cross Route Island
- 2 Westway Travellers Site
- 3 Holland Park Roundabout

D) POCKETS
- 1 Walmer Rd Dead End
- 2 Stable Way Industrial Estate
- 3 Freston Road Dead End
- 4 Bard Road Dead End
- 5 Evesham St Dead End
- 6 Hunt Close
- 7 Queensdale Crescent

Peripheral fragments

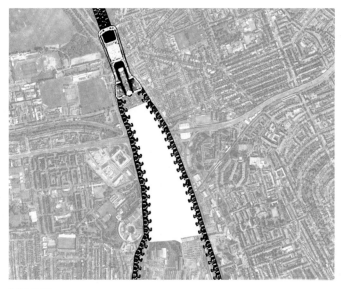

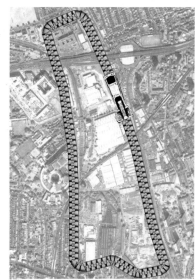

OMA: W12

Despite its central and seemingly well-connected location, the W12 masterplan suffers from local inaccessibility and isolation, as peripheral fragments and desolate strips of redundant spaces left over by large-scale transportation infrastructure have segregated it from the surrounding neighbourhood. Whereas OMA's W12 masterplan intends to resolve this through a central zipping strategy that only creates physical links, this scheme proposes a peripheral zipping through the insertion of a linear arcade that extends Westfield's mall into the masterplan area, so as to consolidate the conflicting edges through programmatic and infrastructural intensification.

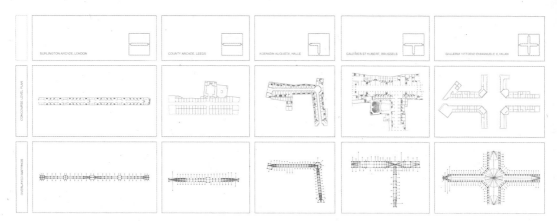

Precedent study: arcade

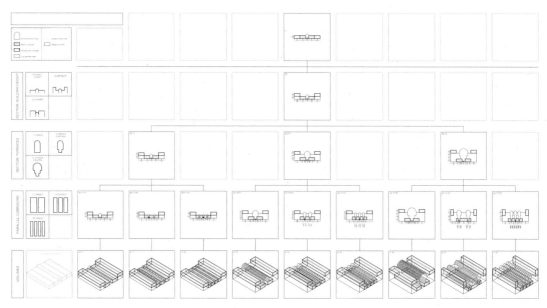

Sectional differentiation

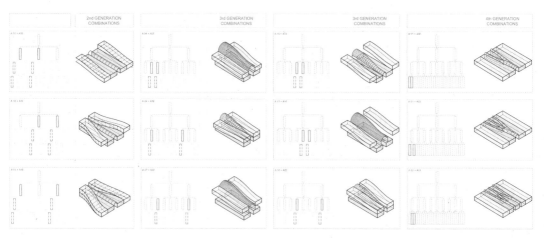

Sectional hybrids

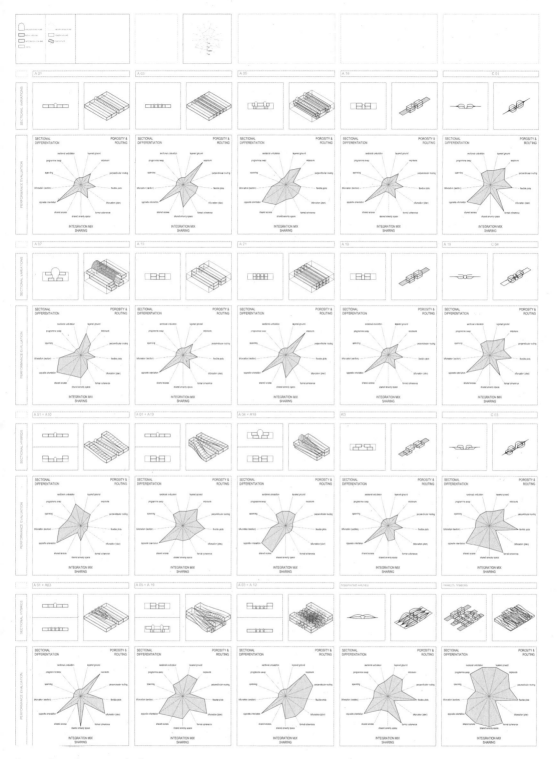

Comparative performance evaluation

Looking at arcade precedents, the type is reduced to its generic sectional organisations, forming a phylogenetic tree of possible variations. By then hybridising and recombining the taxonomised sections, a new planar organisation emerges as a result of

the required transitions between them. These transitions can either be articulated smoothly or as a series of linked structural ribbons.

The subsequent comparative performance analysis allows the definition of potentials

of sectional sequences affecting the ground condition, programmatic and volumetric diversity and circulatory or infrastructural links, resulting in a new sectional taxonomy of either box or strip sections.

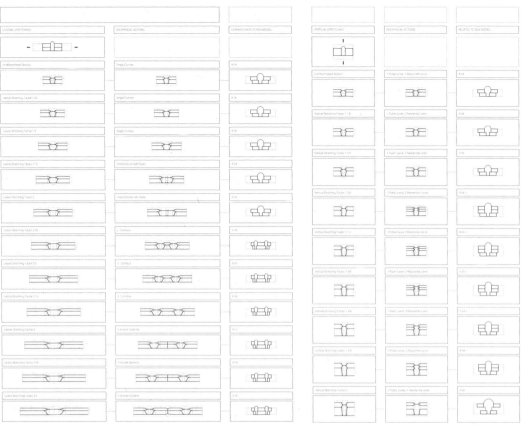

Sectional elasticity

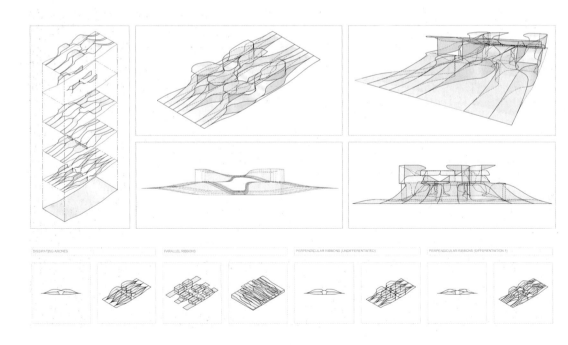

When the generic arcade sections are stretched horizontally or vertically, their elastic behaviour has a reciprocal relationship to potential volume and programme, following the organisational logics of the precedent studies. This can be articulated further through topographical differentiation, leading to the derivation of thickened ground models with structural splines, approaching an arch or dissipating arches, and their resultant ribbon surfaces and volumes. These ribbon modulations create a diversity of spatial and programmatic continuities or separations through weaving either parallel or perpendicular structural strips.

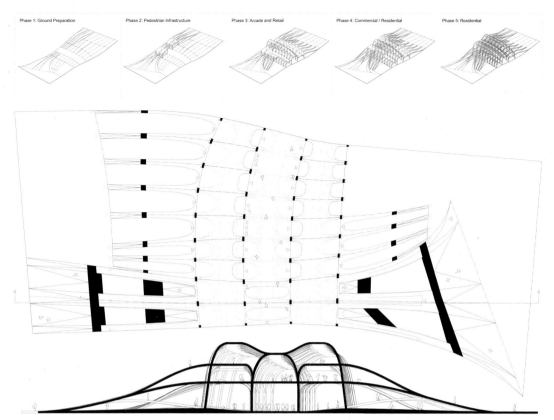

| Phase 1: Ground Preparation | Phase 2: Pedestrian Infrastructure | Phase 3: Arcade and Retail | Phase 4: Commercial / Residential | Phase 5: Residential |

Typical arcade fragment

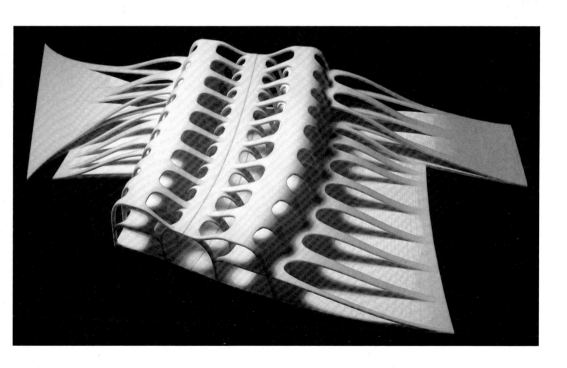

The implementation of the masterplan (shown for a typical segment) consists of the cumulative layering of the arcade system. First the redundant interstitial spaces along the periphery are identified and new pedestrian mobility links determined. Then the foundation is em- bedded into the topographic ground, whereby ground modulations form open public spaces and pedestrian routes. Further infrastructural elements and green link bridges are built, with vertical supports for the susequent ad- dition of the central arcade corridor with its associated retail and commercial activity. Once completed, further layers of housing can be added as required.

LEGEND

residual spaces

merging of fabrics

arcade system

rigs for correlpoints of fluid links

PROGRAMMES EDGES

residential
retail
office
mixed use
leisure
community
healthcare
gastronomical
religious
educational
industrial / storage
studios
pedestrian
transport
green
sports

POTENTIAL FABRIC EXTENSION

residential
retail
office
mixed use
leisure
community
healthcare
gastronomical
religious
educational
industrial / storage
studios
pedestrian
transport
green
sports

Programmatic edge consolidation

52

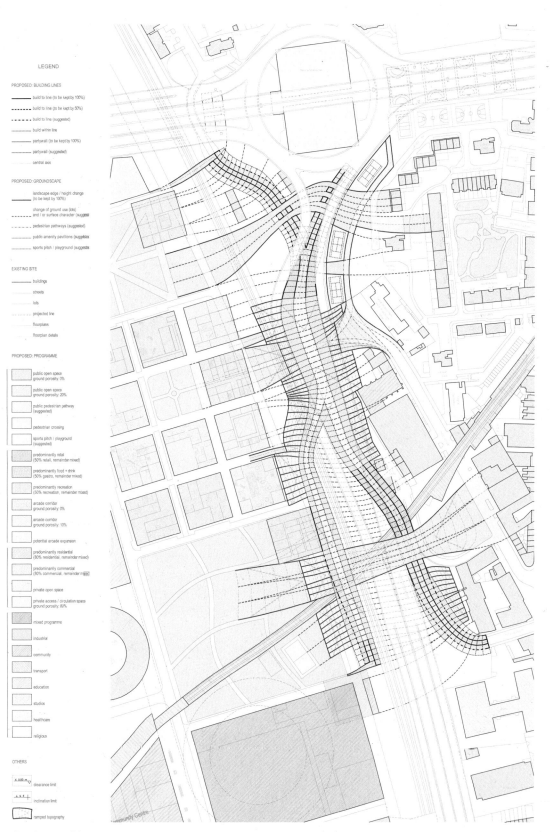

LEGEND

PROPOSED: BUILDING LINES

build to line (to be kept by 100%)
build to line (to be kept by 50%)
build to line (suggested)
build within line
partywall (to be kept by 100%)
partywall (suggested)
central axis

PROPOSED: GROUNDSCAPE

landscape edge / height change
(to be kept by 100%)
change of ground use (lots)
and / or surface character (suggested)
pedestrian pathways (suggested)
public amenity pavilions (suggested)
sports pitch / playground (suggested)

EXISTING SITE

buildings
streets
lots
projected line
floorplans
floorplan details

PROPOSED: PROGRAMME

public open space
ground porosity: 0%
public open space
ground porosity: 20%
public pedestrian pathway
(suggested)
pedestrian crossing
sports pitch / playground
(suggested)
predominantly retail
(50% retail, remainder mixed)
predominantly food + drink
(50% gastro, remainder mixed)
predominantly recreation
(50% recreation, remainder mixed)
arcade corridor
ground porosity: 0%
arcade corridor
ground porosity: 10%
potential arcade expansion
predominantly residential
(80% residential, remainder mixed)
predominantly commercial
(80% commercial, remainder mixed)
private open space
private access / circulation space
ground porosity: 80%
mixed programme
industrial
community
transport
education
studios
healthcare
religious

OTHERS

clearance limit
inclination limit
ramped topography

Community Centre

Urban design guidelines

53

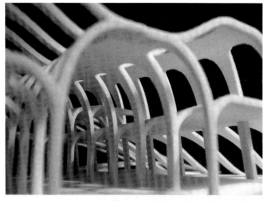

Masterplan model

1.6
RESISTING THE GENERIC EMPIRE
Yicheng Pan

Site: Marina Bay, Singapore

In Singapore, urban planning projects are subject to stringent control by the state. This project resists the formation of a state-engineered 'Generic Empire' – a city of high-rises entirely subjugated to corporate desires – by inverting the skyscraper to provide a typological urban framework that cultivates difference through the coexistence and participation of multiple types and stakeholders.

Marina Bay is a 139-hectare area of reclaimed land that has remained barren for a decade because of the economic crisis in the region. It was relentlessly promoted by the previous government, to no avail; now a new political leadership is trying a different approach, relaunching the original, failed masterplan for the site in a repackaged form, complete with a series of iconic high-rise structures that promise to generate a spectacular skyline. The masterplan proliferates a single building type and stubbornly resists the participation of all other scales, types and investments. The single homogeneous plane of regular blocks can only be occupied by mega-corporations and skyscrapers. As a consequence, the collective public ground plane is forsaken. Lacking the flexibility to involve local establishments and businesses in the development of smaller building types, the site passively awaits huge investments by global corporations.

To subvert the endless proliferation of these skyscrapers across the city grid, this project makes strategic use of the overt political control of urbanism in Singapore. To enforce difference and freedom, it inverts the skyscraper's massing, forcing it to relinquish its control over the ground plane and make way for a multi-layered urban plan. This enables the immediate activation of smaller building types and creates multiple 'clustered' volumes that encourage partnerships between both private and public bodies.

Departing from the state-sponsored, postcard image of a fantasy skyline, the new urban plan of inverted skyscrapers presents an image of perpetual activity, creating an array of differential developmental scales that are less dependent on global economic cycles. Developments can now incrementally begin to form a continuously shaded open space, providing the necessary level of comfort to sustain sociability in Singapore's hot and humid tropical climate.

This project challenges and reconciles issues of control and flexibility in urban planning. It proposes that the best means to sustain difference and participation is not to relinquish control but, conversely, to intensify it.

Type

Type

Masterplan

1960s - present, Public Housing Programme

Masterplan

marina bay 2006, Marina Bay Urban Plan

Promotional Billboard - Urban Renewal Authority

Foreground - Low Rise Developments

Middle ground - Mid Rise Developments

Background - High Rise Developments

Singapore's urban development is closely linked to the will of its political elite. Lee Kuan Yew's Public Housing Programme in the 1960s led to the proliferation of a single type, the slab block, whereas Singapore's current prime minister Lee Hsien Loong now promotes the iconic point block. In this context, Marina Bay's illusory postcard image depends on a completed skyline to depict confidence. As an alternative, this project stages the masterplan image as a series of incremental developments that convey perpetual activity.

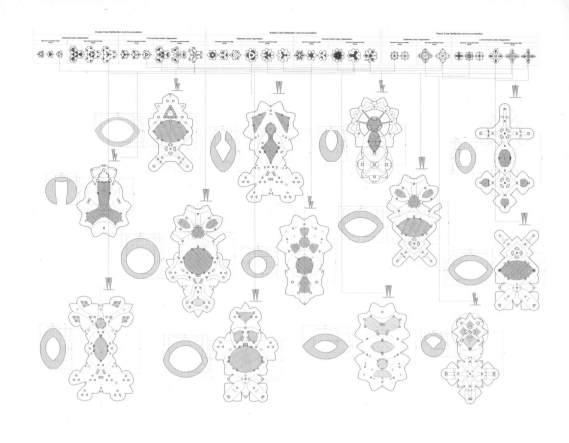

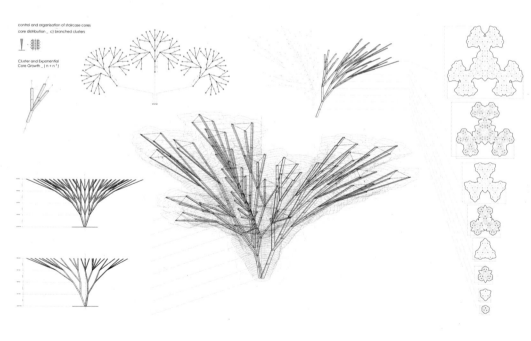

Skyscrapers are controlled by the organisation of the access and staircase cores, which usually results in a ground-dominating podium. By studying the escape core distribution as a single plane – radial incrementally stacked (n+1) or branched cluster with exponential growth (n+3) – the footprint of the skyscraper is minimised and the tower is hollowed out. A variety of new inverted tower typologies emerge and the ground plane is freed up for alternative development.

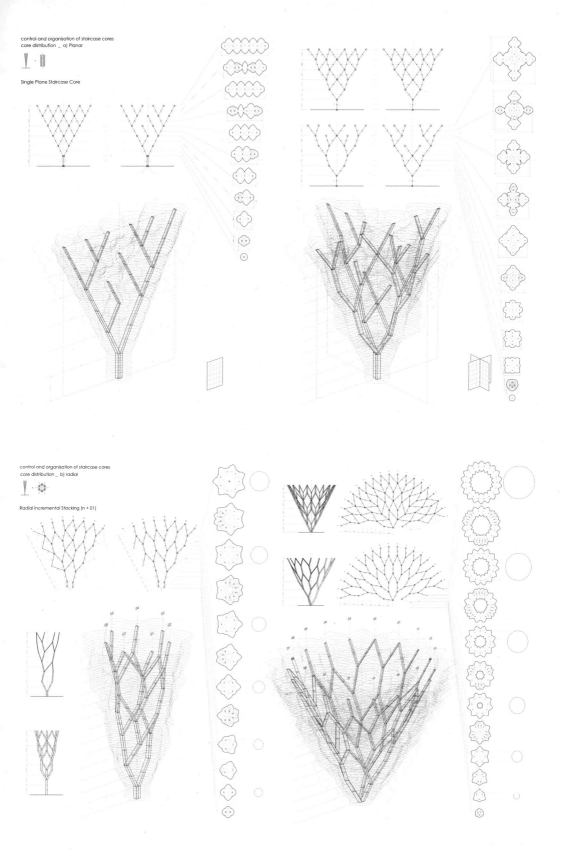

control and organisation of staircase cores
core distribution _ a) Planar

Single Plane Staircase Core

control and organisation of staircase cores
core distribution _ b) radial

Radial Incremental Stacking (n + 01)

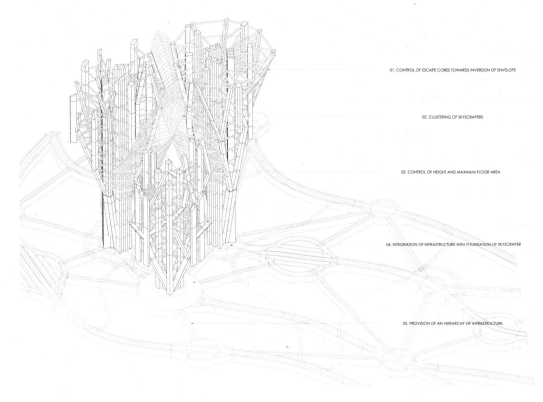

01. CONTROL OF ESCAPE CORES TOWARDS INVERSION OF ENVELOPE

02. CLUSTERING OF SKYSCRAPERS

03. CONTROL OF HEIGHT AND MAXIMUM FLOOR AREA

04. INTEGRATION OF INFRASTRUCTURE WITH FOUNDATION OF SKYSCRAPER

05. PROVISION OF AN HIERARCHY OF INFRASTRUCTURE

Typical skyscraper cluster activating the released ground plane

Cluster model

Skyscraper Floorplates

Inverted Skyscraper Floorplates

Stacked Programme

Dispersed Programme

Extruded Plot Development

Clustered Development of Inverted Skyscraper

Single Land Use Plan

Multi-layered Land Use Plan

Traditional skyscraper and urban design guidelines

Inverted skyscraper and typological guidelines

A typological guideline is written to outline the potential of the inverted skyscraper. Its benefits include the freeing up of the ground plane for diverse and smaller development and investment, usable public spaces within a shaded environment on the ground and a

dispersed instead of stacked programme. For structural efficiency the inverted towers are constructed in clusters of at least three – the intersections between them are designated as privatised public spaces to be maintained by the owner. Controlling the inverted tower

through a series of multiple vertical land-use plans forces programmatic and spatial difference while enabling greater degree of participation and flexibility within the overall masterplan.

Control

Control is relinquished from the urban plane but transferred to the dominant skyscraper type - forcing the skyscraper to relinquish control over the ground plane by controlling it.

the skyscraper is not only controlled via the restriction of the inversed envelope but also the production of multiple urban planes that encompasses public and private programs through the necessity of clustering.

the Control administered hence provides Freedom. - for the Public to activate zones within the skyscraper and smaller stakeholders to activate the ground plane with different types and scale.

Flexibility

the flexibility is afforded not in the planning of the skyscraper but as an urban framework that has the flexibility of absorbing different scale, types and stakeholders, not just on the released ground plane but also within the skyscraper.

within the inversed volume, businesses has the flexibility of taking up differential volumes and providing more than one program on a single plane.

Difference

urbanity do not remain as a single layered urban plane but a set of multi- layered superimposed urban plans.

while the ground plane is released, the diversity of programmatic interaction are elevated higher within the inverted mass of the skyscraper. cultivating difference not only on the ground plane by allowing for other developmental scales and types but also within the skyscraper where programs can interact more freely when no longer mediated by infrastructure.

Participation

with the release of the ground plane, the site can be activated collectively and developed more rapidly through the participation of a wider range of stake holders.

within the skyscraper, there is a possibility for increased public participation through the production of a neutral zone created by overlapping, allowing retail business to be included in the higher levels of the skyscraper and not just restricted to the base of the tower.

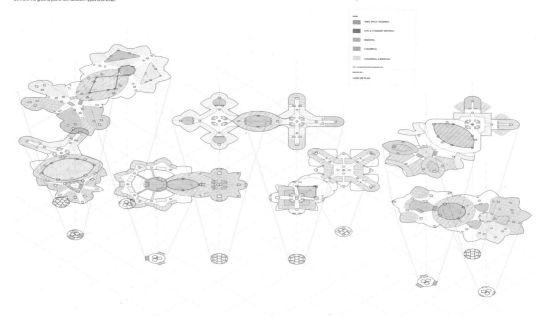

Multi-layered land-use plan for Marina Bay

Multi-layered land-use model

Masterplan model

Control

Through the administration of control on the density and clustering of the inversed skyscrapers, multiple scenerios are generated, allowing each cluster to adopt different strategies of growth according to different economic conditions.

The masterplan achieves freedom as it can simply be planned and phased with starting points of shophouses towards forming the continuous shaded open space. Hence resuscitating the local types while achieving the projected density.

Flexibility

The urban plan gains flexibility by allowing a more spread out and balanced growth, activating zones across the site instead of phasing linearly from one point. The multiple in-built scenerios, from the multiple ground conditions, infrastructural provisions to shading options, allows for the flexibility to absorb a wide range of types and scale of businesses. The urban plan operates flexibly by adopting different strategies of phasing developmnets hence allowing continuous growth regardless of economic cycles.

Difference

Difference is enforced within the skyscraper through the provision of different enveiop sizes, public volumes and dispersal of cores, allowing for a wider range of user groups from private offices to public galleries within the skyscrapers.

The urban plan enforces Difference by promoting the co-existance of multiple types on multiple planes from the resuscitation of the budget shophouse types to the mega investment skyscrapers.

Participation

The urban plan provides for increased participation from local small rage businesses to global corporations through the creation of diverse plot sizes and potentials, multiple scenerios and partnerships.

Fabric Adapting to
Economic Scenerio B

Fabric Adapting to
Economic Scenerio A

MARINA BAY

DE 02

NODE 03

NODE 04

Multi-layered urban plan

64

1.7
MULTIPLE(X)CITY
Bolam Lee

Site: Chonggae Canal, Seoul

Fuelled by industrialisation, Seoul has developed rapidly over the last 30 years, its population increasing tenfold to over ten million. The speed of expansion has given rise to a dense, multi-centred city in a continual state of flux as developers vie to exploit the limited land available.

Chonggaechon, one of the oldest arteries in the heart of the city, typifies this opportunistic redevelopment, which is based on a culture of 'demolish and rebuild'. The site has gone through several reincarnations – originally a canal, it was piled over by a two-tier expressway. Unplanned informal markets flourished in the underbelly of the expressway, forming a continuous mat of commercial fabric across the site. In 2005 the expressway and 'illegal' markets were demolished and the canal restored, ostensibly to provide a new civic amenity, but conveniently paving the way for the creation of a waterfront haven for developers, to be filled with high-rise residential towers and multiplexes.

The proliferation of the multiplex type in Seoul is tied to the growth in demand for leisure facilities following the recovery from the recession of the 1990s and the spread of the five-day working week. The multiplex is a compact container of commerce and culture. It accommodates a spread of commercial operations in the guise of leisure activities: shopping, watching movies, eating, drinking, singing, dancing and even clinics are provided on different floors of a single tower. Its success as the ultimate enclosure of programmes is highly dependent on its programmatic diversity and capacity for renewal. However, a close analysis of its stacked structure reveals a high frequency of renovation and radical changes in programmes in the mid-level zones, making these floors particularly prone to obsolescence. At the same time the blank building enclosure and interiorised circulation routes – which are deliberately disconnected from the urban context – prevent the growth of other forms of leisure activity and accelerate the multiplex's own deterioration, creating urban blanks in the heart of the city.

The strategy of this project is to minimise the redundant zones of the multiplex and reinhabit these urban voids by forcing a typological change. The waist of the type is 'pinched' to create an hourglass-like distribution of volumes: within this, areas unsuitable for shopping use can be converted into potential public volumes – a new type of vertical open space. On the ground, the multiplex is transformed into a robust connector, creating new links with surrounding fabric. Sliding the pinching point up and down allows flexibility in the way the tower touches the ground. The footprint can be minimised to preserve the existing fabric, where this is desirable.

Instead of ignoring the multiplex – which continues to be the dominant type in the redevelopment of Seoul – this project attempts to define an alternative model for the type that can contribute to the city by setting up connections on the ground plane and bringing the public realm inside. This is achieved by exploiting the inherent redundancy of the present multiplex type to provide the city with the open spaces that it lacks after decades of extreme over-development. These vertical open spaces can become the multiplied grounds for the growth of an alternative leisure activity, one that is not defined by commercial activity or the desire of developers to make a profit.

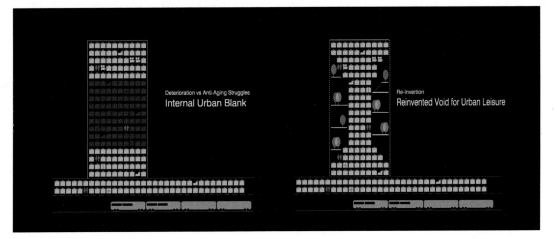

Deterioration vs Anti-Aging Struggles
Internal Urban Blank

Re-Invertion
Reinvented Void for Urban Leisure

In response to an increasing demand for leisure, infrastructural nodes in Seoul are dominated by multiplexes. These types, deliberately disconnected from the urban context, offer no possibilities for local or diversified forms of leisure, which accelerates their expiry. By pinching the waist and so minimising the most redundant zones of the multiplex, potentially public volumes are created, giving the interiorised model of the multiplex a possible exterior interface.

Growth of Seoul (1958-1990)

Growth of Retail Types

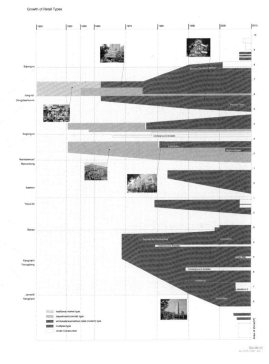

Urban and multiplex growth

1960

1967

1976

1990

2006

History of Chonggae

Existing spatial organisation of multiplex

The stacked model of the homogeneous multiplex tower is omnipresent in Seoul. Though it ostensibly offers a variety of leisure activities, it is functionally mono-programmatic: leisure as shopping.

Renovations and radical changes of programme occur most frequently in the mid-level zones, making them most susceptible to redundancy.

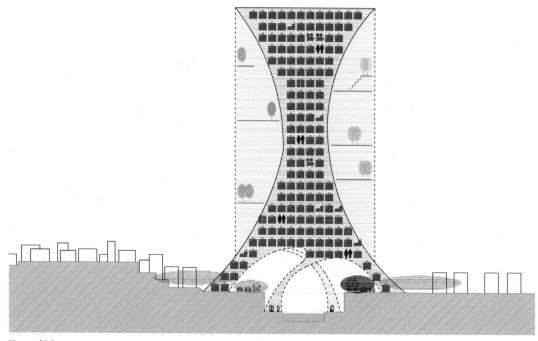

New multiplex type

The multiplex is transformed from a rigid interiorised type into a connector joining the local fabric with the new canal development.

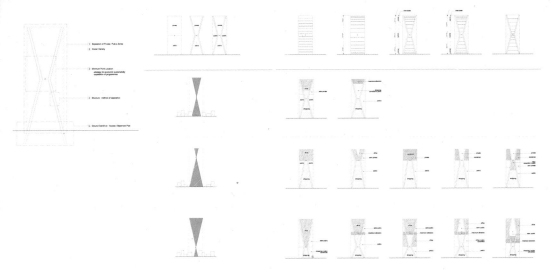

Internal organisation

Structural models

The 'pinching' of the tower results in a hyperboloid structure that can be articulated through three distinct models: straight, tessellated or branched tower.

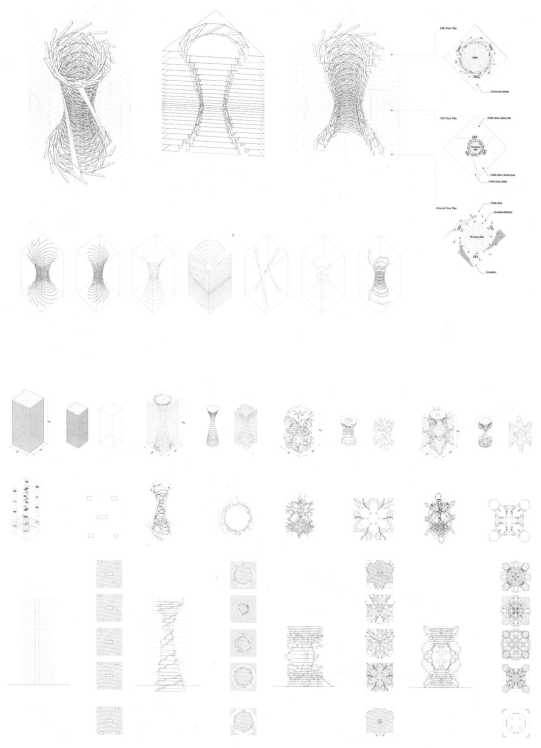

Closed space/spiral model

The internal organisation and distribution of public volumes varies depending on the structural model. The closed space or spiral model provides clearly separated atrium spaces with a hierarchical distribution. The open space or branched model, however, gives a higher degree of connectivity between public and private zones by establishing a differential network of circulation.

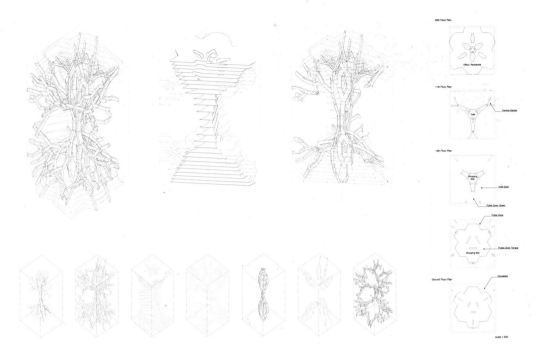

Open space/branched model

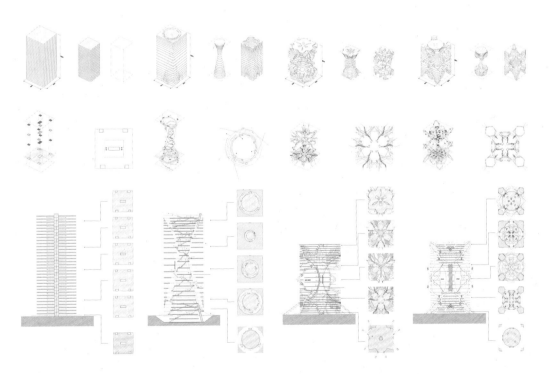

Model comparison

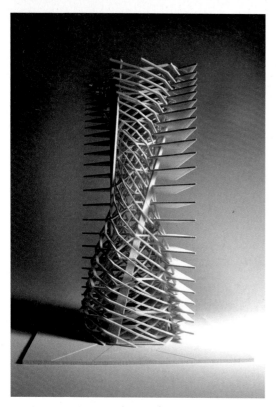
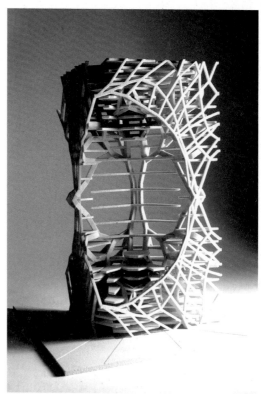

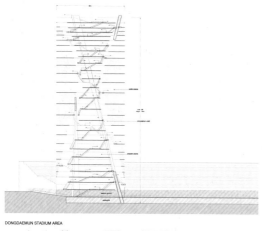

DONGDAEMUN STADIUM AREA

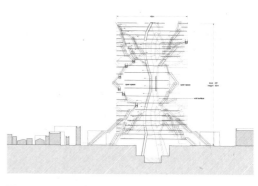

GREENPOINT 2 : RECONNECTION OF WHOLESALE MALLS [AV / ANTIQUE / KITCHEN EQUIP.]

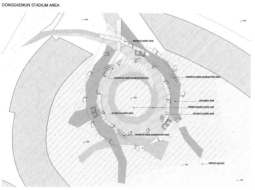

Typical fragment

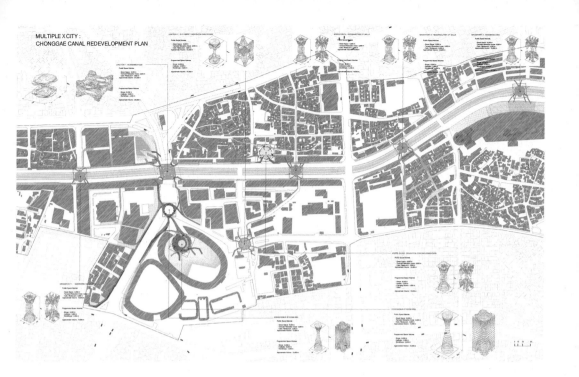

MULTIPLE X CITY :
CHONGGAE CANAL REDEVELOPMENT PLAN

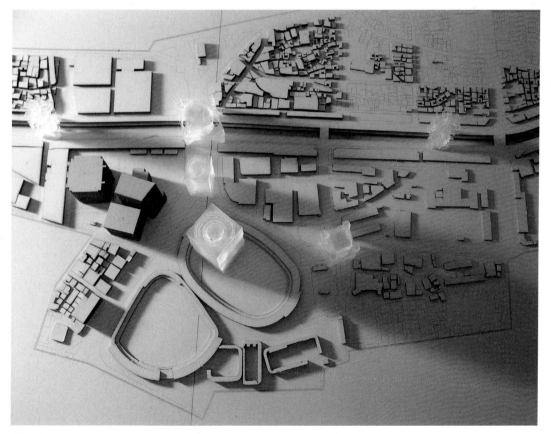

Urban plan

1.8
GENETICALLY MODIFIED TERRACE HOUSE
Martin Jameson

Site: Blackpool, UK

In its heyday Blackpool was one of the most successful leisure cities of the twentieth century. A potent mix of bawdy music-hall entertainment, spectacular amusement rides and a long sandy beach brought in 17 million visitors a year. However, the advent of cheap air travel has seen Blackpool slip into decay, turning it into a shrinking city.

The town can be analysed through a series of failing building types in disrepair: the famous guesthouses are now filled with families on state benefits, the amusement arcades are virtually empty, and the once grand Victorian hotels are no longer able to attract guests.

On account of this decay, Blackpool has attracted considerable government attention and funding. A series of masterplans has been drawn up, based on the assumption that the city can continue its role as a holiday resort marketed by spectacular amusements and attractions.

The existing EDAW/Jerde masterplan divides the entertainment part of the town into four zones, each with a particular focus: shopping, attractions and rides, guesthouses, and casinos. This strategy reinforces the current programmatic divisions, and inflexibility, of the town. The Gensler plan proposes a monolithic integrated resort within the supercasino site, inwardly focused and oriented to visiting tourists only.

As an alternative, this project rejects the traditional reliance on tourism and instead proposes the modified terraced house as a source of regeneration that provides new housing stock and encourages a resident population whilst absorbing leisure activities within its new type and urban fabric.

The terraced house, the dominant type of Blackpool, was adapted during the twentieth century to take on the role of guesthouse. The typological challenge now is to redefine this type as an elastic envelope that can accommodate differing spatial requirements, ranging from housing and guesthouse accommodation to commercial use and the large-scale demands of casinos and entertainment programmes. The party walls and internal circulation are manipulated to regulate the building sections and plans and, with this, the boundaries of privacy – allowing the close proximity of otherwise opposed programmes.

The new type is characterised both by differential spatial configurations – the use of courtyards, light-wells, recessed spaces – and by structural features, for example, the use of staircases or ramped circulation to support cantilevered decks and green spaces.

The terrace block itself is based on subtle transitions between varying terrace types. This not only incorporates difference and variety but also allows for the accommodation of new programmes over time. Much like the adapted terrace house, the new urban fabric is capable of combining varying levels of privacy. Instead of streets, it is formed of a series of islands that establish enclaves of privacy in a system of public activity.

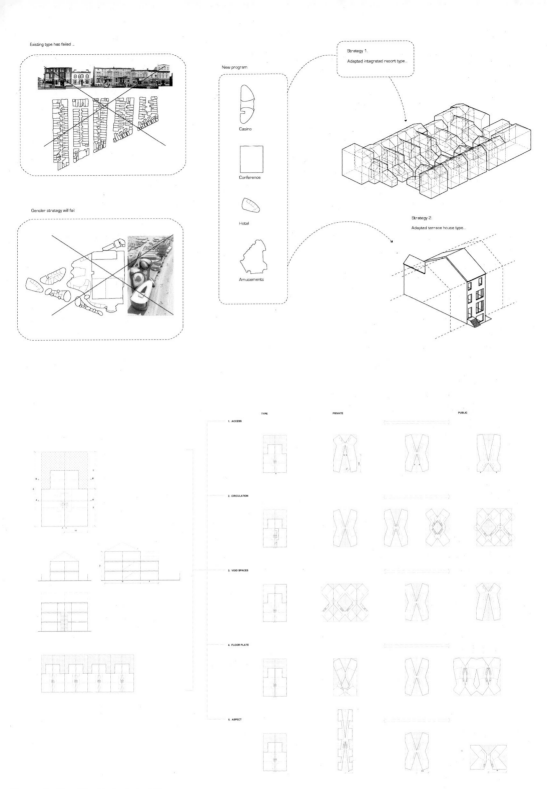

Party wall split and front-to-back circulation

The challenge for Blackpool is to address the problem of the shrinking city and to focus on a resident population. The types that make up typical failed fragments are dominated by terraced houses and need to be rethought to adapt to and absorb new leisure activities. The terrace type is characterised by its elastic section: to unfold typological richness, the circulation is horizontally and vertically linked and the party wall split. This allows for a wide range of new interior organisations and the control of privacy and adjacency.

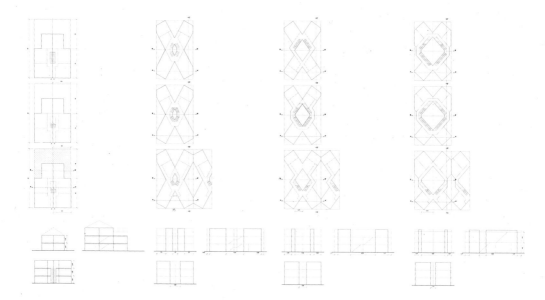

Manipulating the crossover

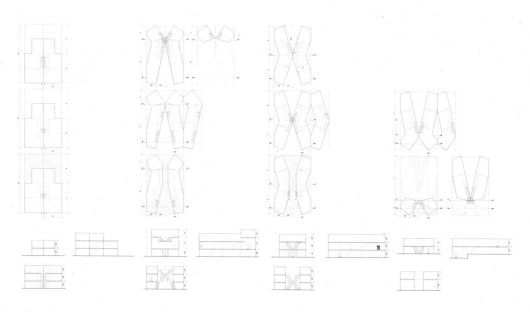

Manipulating the meeting point

Splitting open the party wall and linking the
circulation creates a radically more flexible
type with a wide range of performative
characteristics.

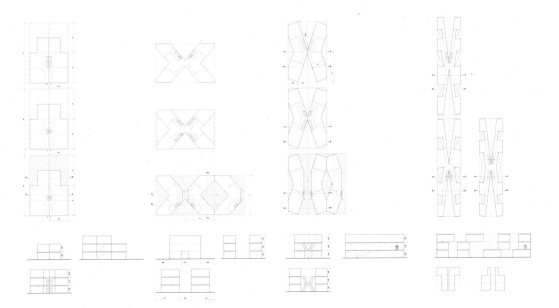

Manipulating the frontage

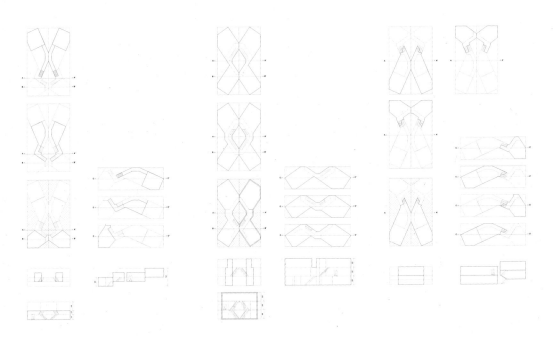

Combined operations

These operations allow different degrees
of public and private programme through
the creation of courtyards, recessed spaces,
linked circulation, cantilevered sections, etc.

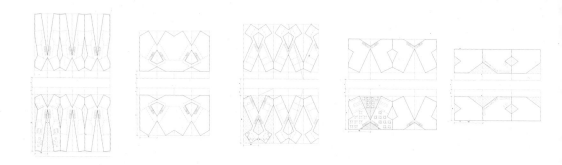

Terrace base types

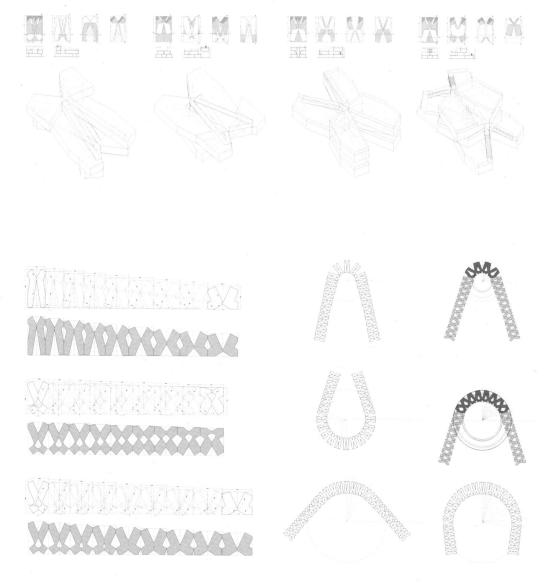

Site adaptation

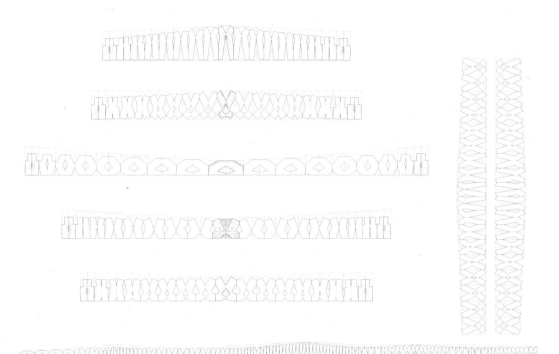

Formal blending

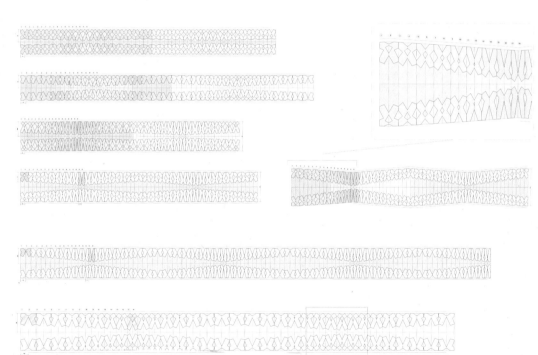

Programmatic blending

The terraced house streetscape is formed
by the formal and programmatic blending
of existing and proposed or required
types/buildings to accommodate the new
masterplan for Blackpool – with a focus on
regeneration through housing provision.

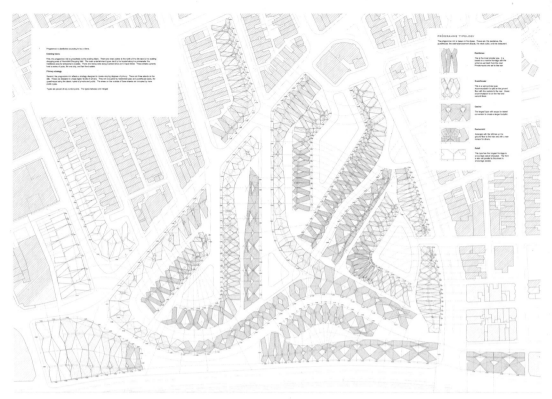

Programme distribution

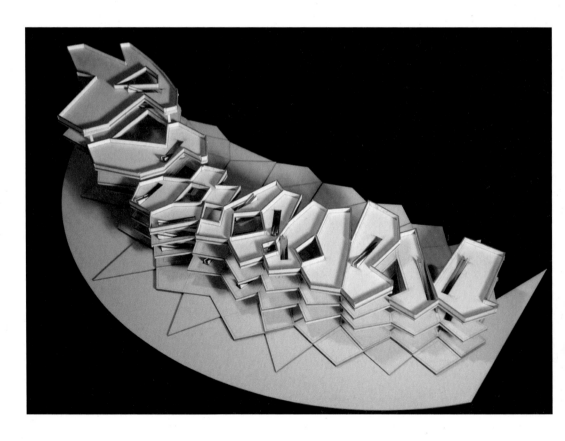

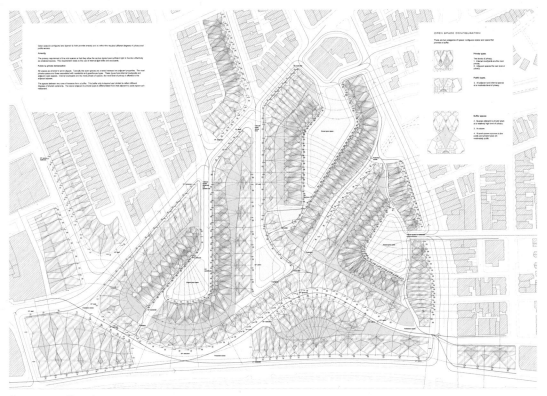

Open space configuration

1.9
OPEN SOURCE FABRIC
Max von Werz

Site: Zorrozaurre, Bilbao

The potential of a masterplan to promote new industries should not rely on the increasingly predictable strategy of engaging star architects as image-makers. In the context of Bilbao's dwindling leisure economy, 'Open Source Fabric' rethinks type as a permissive fabric of the urban block and uses the differentiation of external collective voids as a mechanism to absorb relentless shifts in the knowledge industry. Resisting the trend for singular types of innovation environments, this project introduces diverse type-specific environments that are capable of consolidating synergetic leisure networks, so as to encourage a renewed dynamic of lived-in population in the confined peninsula of Zorrozaurre.

As the Guggenheim's novelty factor wears off it is questionable how long the 'Bilbao Effect' can be sustained. Zorrozaurre, a 60-hectare peninsula in the city centre, has been chosen to spearhead the transition towards new industries and revitalise the post-industrial waterfront. The choice of Zaha Hadid as the masterplanner is a clear continuation of Bilbao's strategy of reinvention, whereby star architects are hired to lubricate global PR machineries and ensure the success of any proposed industry. Despite the formal vision and scenography of the masterplan, its success will be dependent on its ability to absorb changes within industries while providing specific research building types and a vibrant urban realm.

Within the contemporary discourse of research environments, a dichotomy has been established: the suburban technopark vs the inner city technopole. The former offers an extreme degree of typological specificity, but these interiorised building types are completely oblivious to their surrounding context. The latter makes use of an existing vibrant public realm but relinquishes control over building types. Both models are ultimately imperfect and, favouring neither, this project attempts to compress the whole gradient of research environments – from city centres to their suburbs – onto the peninsula. Multiple dense technopole centres with synergetic links to adjacent neighbourhoods are envisioned – each catering to a different industry and dispersing outwards to loose technopark peripheries. This mediation attempts to resist the tendency for singular visions and reinforces the resilience of the urban plan by accommodating unforeseen fluctuations in the leisure and knowledge industries.

Following a typological investigation of research buildings, the project set out to create an open-source menu of urban blocks acting as a toolbox from which anyone could generate a diverse yet coherent urban fabric, liberating the future city from the tyranny of the single masterplan vision. However, the array of endless options created a condition that can best be described as a form of democratic paralysis. This led to the realisation that a certain degree of top-down strategic control over the principal distribution of concentration is necessary as a framework to unleash typological difference. The potential of a polycentric radial grid to transform the urban block and its associative open space is thus exploited, creating centres of synergetic intensity and a loose periphery responding to Bilbao's urgent need for spaces of leisure and outdoor activity.

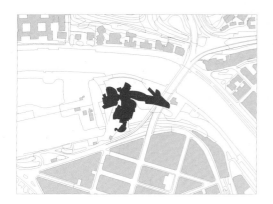 

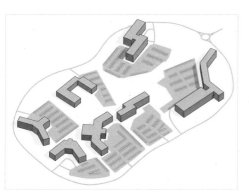 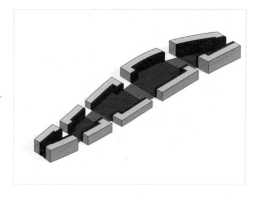

Charged void

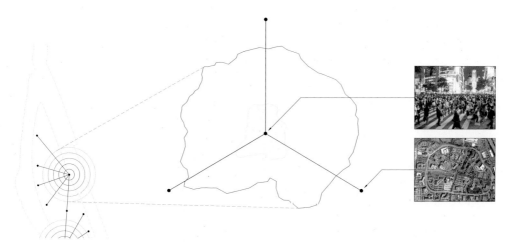

Compression of city Model

What comes after the 'Bilbao Effect'? The example of Zorrozaurre offers the opportunity to rethink the peninsula as a leisure fabric attracting new patterns of urban living. The figure-ground argument is relevant to the discourse of research environments, and multiple dense technopole centres can be envisioned – each catering to a different industry and dispersing outwards towards loose technopark peripherics. This mediation attempts to resist the tendency for singular visions and reinforces the resilience of the urban plan by facilitating unforeseen fluctuations in the leisure and knowledge industries.

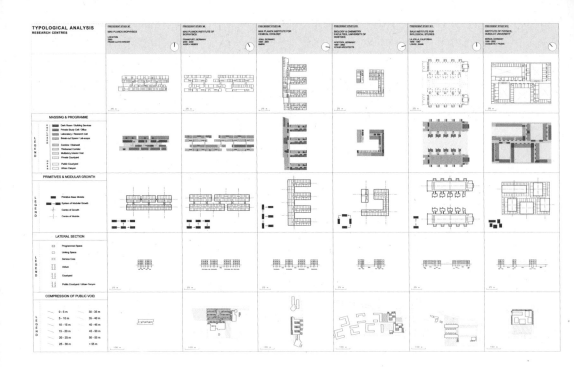

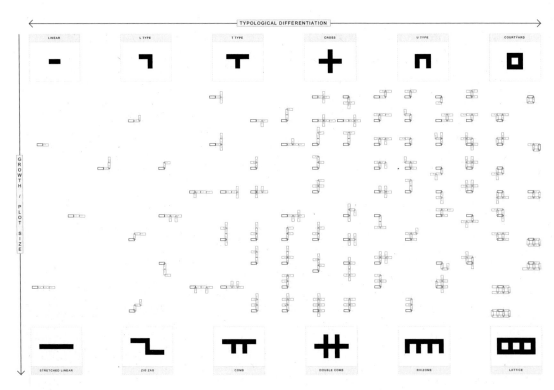

Taxonomy of new base types

Research environments, and in particular laboratories, rely on very specific building types. Throughout the development of these types, voids have regulated the degree of communication and the exchange of ideas. These voids are predominantly interior, ranging from thickened corridors and break-out spaces to courtyards and atria.

Most research types can be broken down to elemental linear slab modules which are plugged together to allow an infinite variety of configurations. From this one can derive a standardised modular grid and spatial dimensions.

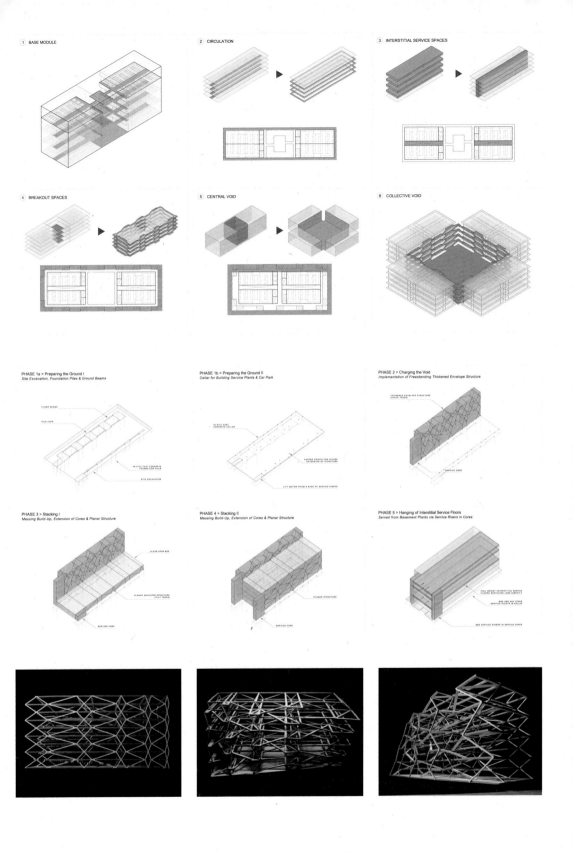

1 BASE MODULE

2 CIRCULATION

3 INTERSTITIAL SERVICE SPACES

4 BREAKOUT SPACES

5 CENTRAL VOID

6 COLLECTIVE VOID

PHASE 1a > Preparing the Ground I
Site Excavation, Foundation Piles & Ground Beams

PHASE 1b > Preparing the Ground II
Cellar for Building Service Plants & Car Park

PHASE 2 > Charging the Void
Implementation of Freestanding Thickened Envelope Structure

PHASE 3 > Stacking I
Massing Build-Up, Extension of Cores & Planar Structure

PHASE 4 > Stacking II
Massing Build-Up, Extension of Cores & Planar Structure

PHASE 5 > Hanging of Interstitial Service Floors
Served from Basement Plants via Service Risers in Cores

The generic linear slab module is turned inside out by externalising circulation spaces, structure and services in the form of a thickened habitable building envelope that regulates and programmatically and visually charges the urban void. What was once a singular interiorised type becomes a collective urban fabric.

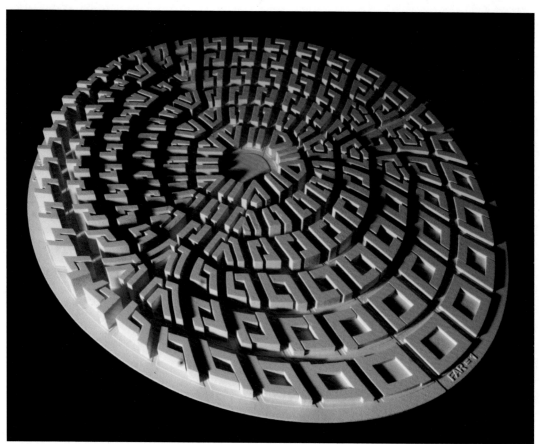

Transition between base types

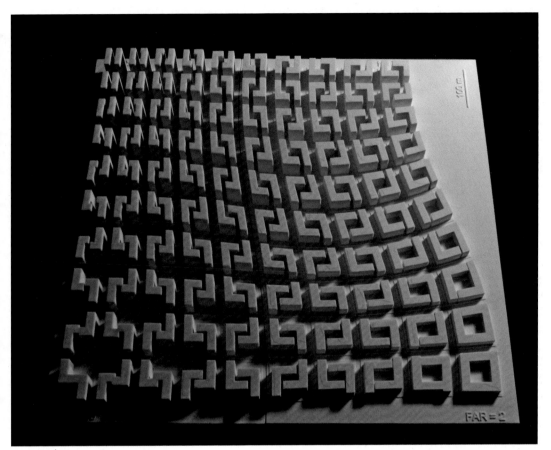

Sectional differentiation of the urban block

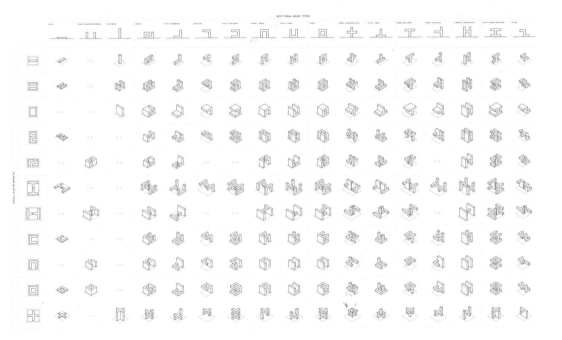

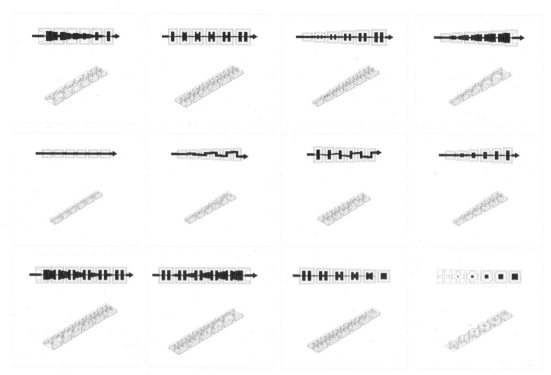

Leisure routes through fabric ribbons

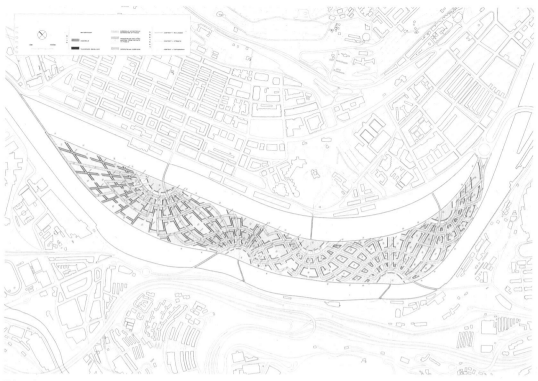

Urban plan

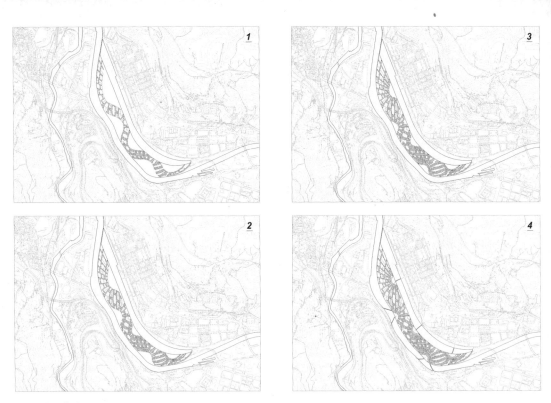

Construction phasing

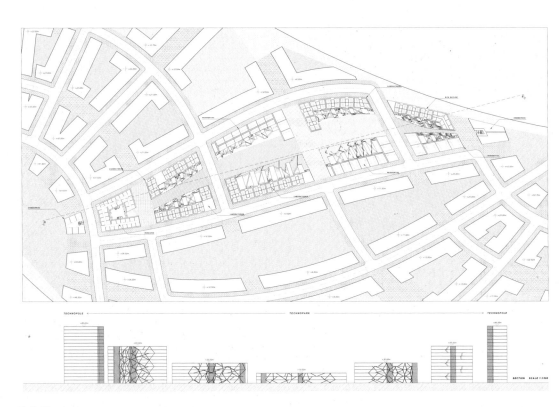

Typical fragment

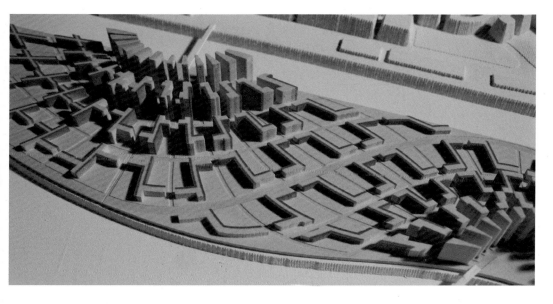

2.0
FIGURING

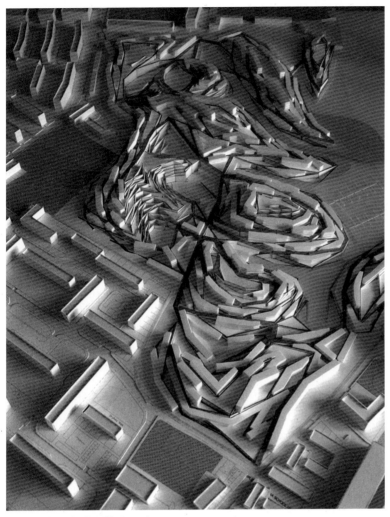

Minseok Kim, Multiple Public Ground

2.1
HYDROLOGICAL FABRIC
Dan Narita

Site: Lea Valley, London

The hydrotype, a hybrid of water-processing typologies and sports architecture, provides the primary remedial infrastructure for implementing this strategic sustainable masterplan for the Lea Valley Olympic site.

The project developed as a critique of the existing Olympic masterplan, which has no integrated environmental strategy for urban renewal and sensitive land-use patterns. As an alternative approach, it defines a distribution system of new urban programmes in response to toxicity levels in the existing soil and ground-water. A time-based strategy for the gradual decontamination of the land is then synchronised with the phasing of a new urban centre in the Lea Valley.

The existing soil is replaced with an adaptive foundation system with a highly differentiated layout: the foundation piles have different depths (and therefore different load-bearing capacities) depending on the requirements for decontamination. This strategic installation of a new ground implies an adaptive zoning of new developments, where the future urban massing is determined by its capacity to support diverse building heights and types. Thus the contamination map and the proposed masterplan are reciprocal and provide a direct and environmentally considered foundation masterplan that regulates possible development.

Decontamination is achieved over a period of 20 years. Initially the hydrotypes are located in the future Olympic sites, which are defined as high-risk contamination zones with the deepest foundations and the largest capacity to absorb programme. Each of the Olympic sites first undergoes a process of soil excavation and redistribution, followed by the installation of special foundation piles and caps. Only then can the site be configured and organised according to the development plans. Varying the organisation of the piling grid produces a range of formal and volumetric plot articulations that can be tailored to respond to varying requirements.

The first phase of decontamination also frees up additional sites within the Lea Valley for future development. By using the contamination levels as a guide for densification, a highly differentiated juxtaposition of urban types and hydrotypes can be envisioned, creating differentiated hydrological fabrics.

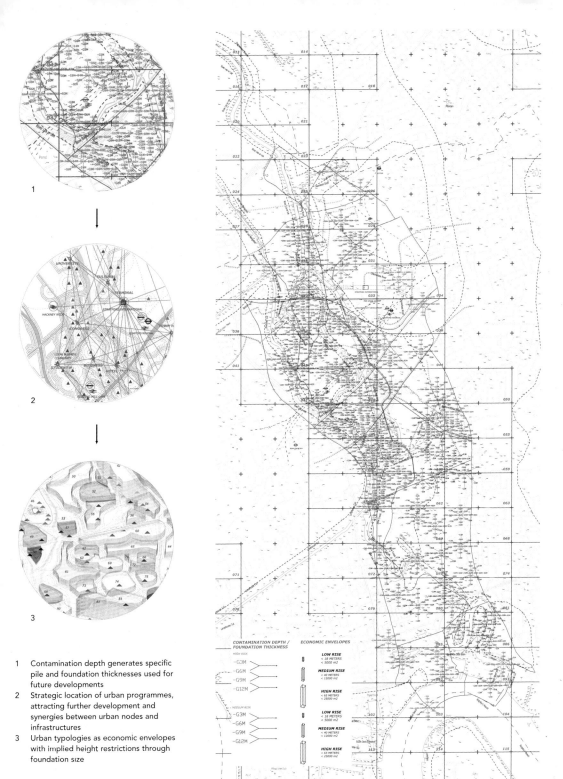

1 Contamination depth generates specific
   pile and foundation thicknesses used for
   future developments
2 Strategic location of urban programmes,
   attracting further development and
   synergies between urban nodes and
   infrastructures
3 Urban typologies as economic envelopes
   with implied height restrictions through
   foundation size

Contamination depth map

Foundation as Development Opportunity:
The London Development Agency (LDA) is not
responsible for building the new foundation
ground system within the masterplan area.
All developers have to ensure a minimum
foundation thickness determined by the risk of
pollution in the existing contaminated soil.

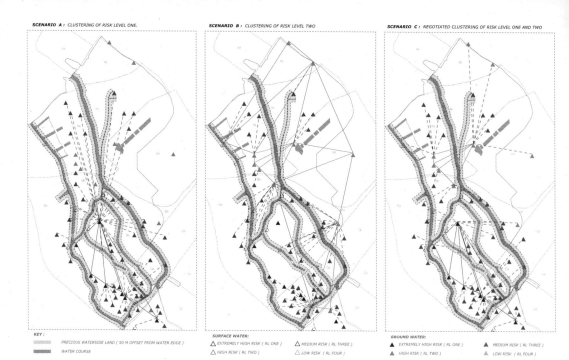

SCENARIO A : CLUSTERING OF RISK LEVEL ONE.　　SCENARIO B : CLUSTERING OF RISK LEVEL TWO　　SCENARIO C : NEGOTIATED CLUSTERING OF RISK LEVEL ONE AND TWO

KEY :

▨ PRECIOUS WATERSIDE LAND (50 M OFFSET FROM WATER EDGE)

▨ WATER COURSE

SURFACE WATER:

△ EXTREMELY HIGH RISK (RL ONE)　　△ MEDIUM RISK (RL THREE)

△ HIGH RISK (RL TWO)　　△ LOW RISK (RL FOUR)

GROUND WATER:

▲ EXTREMELY HIGH RISK (RL ONE)　　▲ MEDIUM RISK (RL THREE)

▲ HIGH RISK (RL TWO)　　▲ LOW RISK (RL FOUR)

Site clustering

1　Contamination map
Contaminated clusters are networked to
identify sites of initial implementation.

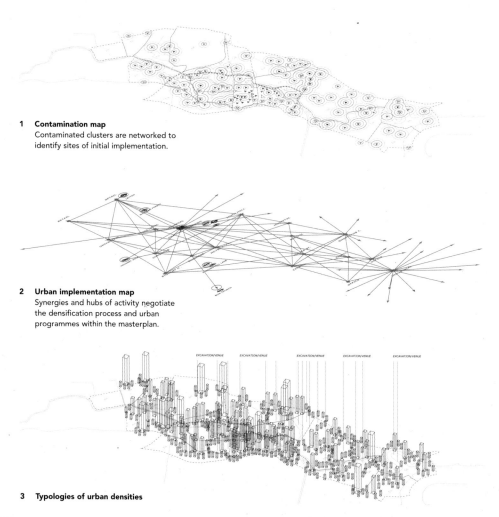

2　Urban implementation map
Synergies and hubs of activity negotiate
the densification process and urban
programmes within the masterplan.

3　Typologies of urban densities

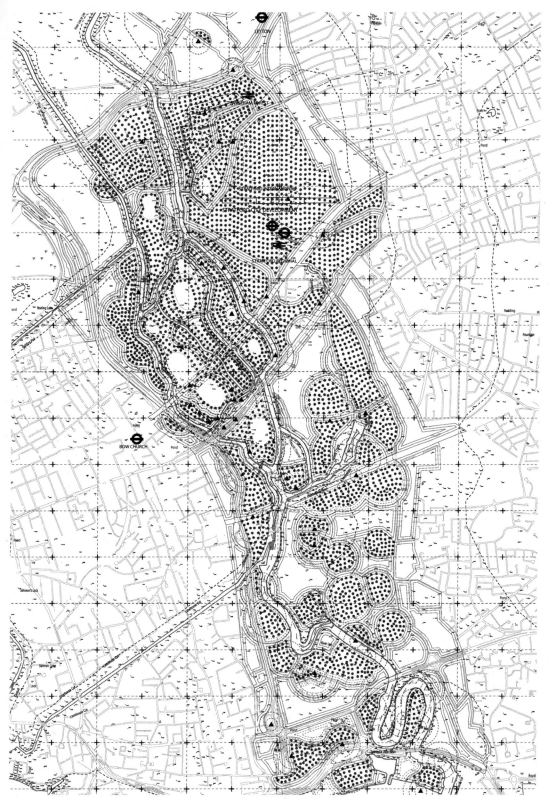

Foundation masterplan

White zones are extremely high-risk areas that require excavation and subsequent soil redistribution, but also have the greatest potential to absorb physical structures. This is where the Olympic venues are inserted, after the hydrotypes (water purification and decontamination plants) have decontaminated the soil and environment.

All other sites are at low risk of contamination and ready for immediate development and ground preparation starts with flexible foundation piles and caps.

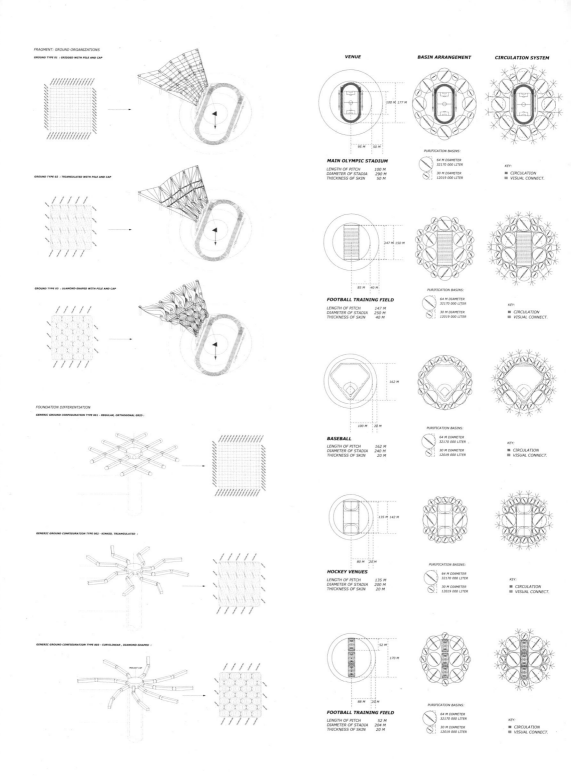

FRAGMENT: GROUND ORGANIZATIONS

GROUND TYPE 01 : GRIDDED WITH PILE AND CAP

GROUND TYPE 02 : TRIANGULATED WITH PILE AND CAP

GROUND TYPE 03 : DIAMOND-SHAPED WITH PILE AND CAP

FOUNDATION DIFFERENTIATION

GENERIC GROUND CONFIGURATION TYPE 001 – REGULAR, ORTHOGONAL GRID :

GENERIC GROUND CONFIGURATION TYPE 002 – KINKED, TRIANGULATED :

GENERIC GROUND CONFIGURATION TYPE 003 – CURVILINEAR , DIAMOND-SHAPED :

| VENUE | BASIN ARRANGEMENT | CIRCULATION SYSTEM |

MAIN OLYMPIC STADIUM

LENGTH OF PITCH	100 M
DIAMETER OF STADIA	290 M
THICKNESS OF SKIN	50 M

PURIFICATION BASINS:
64 M DIAMETER 32170 000 LITER
30 M DIAMETER 12019 000 LITER

KEY:
■ CIRCULATION
■ VISUAL CONNECT.

FOOTBALL TRAINING FIELD

LENGTH OF PITCH	147 M
DIAMETER OF STADIA	250 M
THICKNESS OF SKIN	40 M

PURIFICATION BASINS:
64 M DIAMETER 32170 000 LITER
30 M DIAMETER 12019 000 LITER

KEY:
■ CIRCULATION
■ VISUAL CONNECT.

BASEBALL

LENGTH OF PITCH	162 M
DIAMETER OF STADIA	240 M
THICKNESS OF SKIN	20 M

PURIFICATION BASINS:
64 M DIAMETER 32170 000 LITER
30 M DIAMETER 12019 000 LITER

KEY:
■ CIRCULATION
■ VISUAL CONNECT.

HOCKEY VENUES

LENGTH OF PITCH	135 M
DIAMETER OF STADIA	200 M
THICKNESS OF SKIN	20 M

PURIFICATION BASINS:
64 M DIAMETER 32170 000 LITER
30 M DIAMETER 12019 000 LITER

KEY:
■ CIRCULATION
■ VISUAL CONNECT.

FOOTBALL TRAINING FIELD

LENGTH OF PITCH	52 M
DIAMETER OF STADIA	204 M
THICKNESS OF SKIN	20 M

PURIFICATION BASINS:
64 M DIAMETER 32170 000 LITER
30 M DIAMETER 12019 000 LITER

KEY:
■ CIRCULATION
■ VISUAL CONNECT.

The foundation masterplan can be interpreted in different ways depending on the developer's/ architect's needs and design. For example, a gridded, triangulated or diamond-shaped structural pile and beam system can be used, resulting in a varied spatial and architectural articulation. At the same time, the Olympic sites (networked high-risk zones) require a series of specific sports structure and hydrotype clusters.

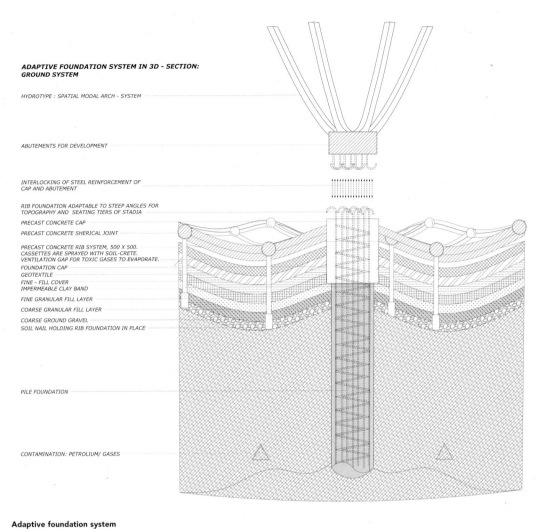

**ADAPTIVE FOUNDATION SYSTEM IN 3D - SECTION:
GROUND SYSTEM**

HYDROTYPE : SPATIAL MODAL ARCH - SYSTEM

ABUTEMENTS FOR DEVELOPMENT

INTERLOCKING OF STEEL REINFORCEMENT OF
CAP AND ABUTEMENT

RIB FOUNDATION ADAPTABLE TO STEEP ANGLES FOR
TOPOGRAPHY AND SEATING TIERS OF STADIA

PRECAST CONCRETE CAP

PRECAST CONCRETE SHERICAL JOINT

PRECAST CONCRETE RIB SYSTEM, 500 X 500.
CASSETTES ARE SPRAYED WITH SOIL-CRETE.
VENTILATION GAP FOR TOXIC GASES TO EVAPORATE.
FOUNDATION CAP
GEOTEXTILE
FINE - FILL COVER
IMPERMEABLE CLAY BAND

FINE GRANULAR FILL LAYER

COARSE GRANULAR FILL LAYER

COARSE GROUND GRAVEL
SOIL NAIL HOLDING RIB FOUNDATION IN PLACE

PILE FOUNDATION

CONTAMINATION: PETROLIUM/ GASES

Adaptive foundation system
Piles and caps

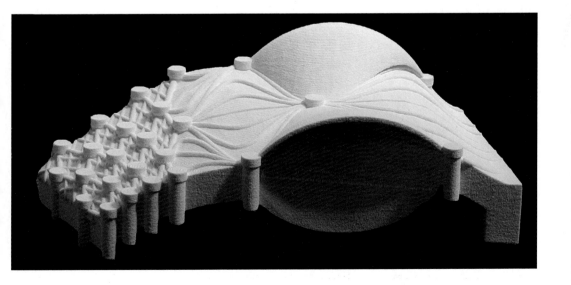

RELATIONSHIP 001:

MAIN PUBLIC CIRCULATION ROUTES ARE INHERITED FORM THE OLYMPIC CIRCULATION ROUTES. THEY ARE BOTH VEHICULAR AND PEDESTRIAN.

INTERNAL PATHWAYS

RELATIONSHIP 002:

INTERNAL CIRCULATION ROUTES DEPART FROM THE MAIN PUBLIC ROAD. INTERNAL ROUTES ALSO ACT AS LINKS BETWEEN MAIN PUBLIC CIRCULATION AND OPEN PUBLIC SPACES.

ACCESSIBILITY/ COVERED PATHWAYS/ ROOF PATHWAYS

RELATIONSHIP 003:

EACH UNIT HAS ACCESS POINTS TO MAIN ROAD AND OPEN SPACE. PATHWAYS ARE COVERED WHERE BUILD VOLUME IS RAISED FOR PURIFICATION BASIN OR WATER STORAGE TOWER. IN TIGHT AREAS OF LAND PUBLIC CIRCULATION IS PLACED ABOVE BUILD VOLUME.

OFFICE / RETAIL

RELATIONSHIP 004:

OFFICE UNITS ARE PLACED AROUND CENTRAL OPEN SPACE. SOME RETAIL UNITS ARE SUPPLIED TO SERVE OFFICE WORKERS. RETAIL UNITS ARE PLACES IN SMALLER LINEAR STRETCH OF LAND TO BECOME A SHOPPING BOULEVARD.

WATER PURIFICATION

RELATIONSHIP 005:

PURIFICATION BASINS ARE PLACED IN OFFICE AREA BECAUSE UNITS ARE LARGER AND HAVE A GREATER ABSORPTION CAPACITY.

WATER STORAGE

RELATIONSHIP 006:

WATER TOWERS ARE PLACED ON SMALLER UNITS BUT THEY WILL GROW IN HIGHT TO ABSORB WATER, SUPPLY THE SMALL LOCALBUSINESS COMMUNITY AND MORE.

ADMINISTRATIVE BUILDING FOR WATER MANAGEMENT

RELATIONSHIP 007:

ADMINISTRATIVE BUILDING IS PLACED CENTRALLY TO OVERSEE AND MONITOR THE PURIFICATION BASINS.

BUFFER ZONES

RELATIONSHIP 008:

CENTRAL OPEN SPACE AND LINEAR RECREATIONAL OPEN SPACE CAN ALSO BE USED AS A MARKET PLACE OR SPORTS OR CULTURAL GROUND.

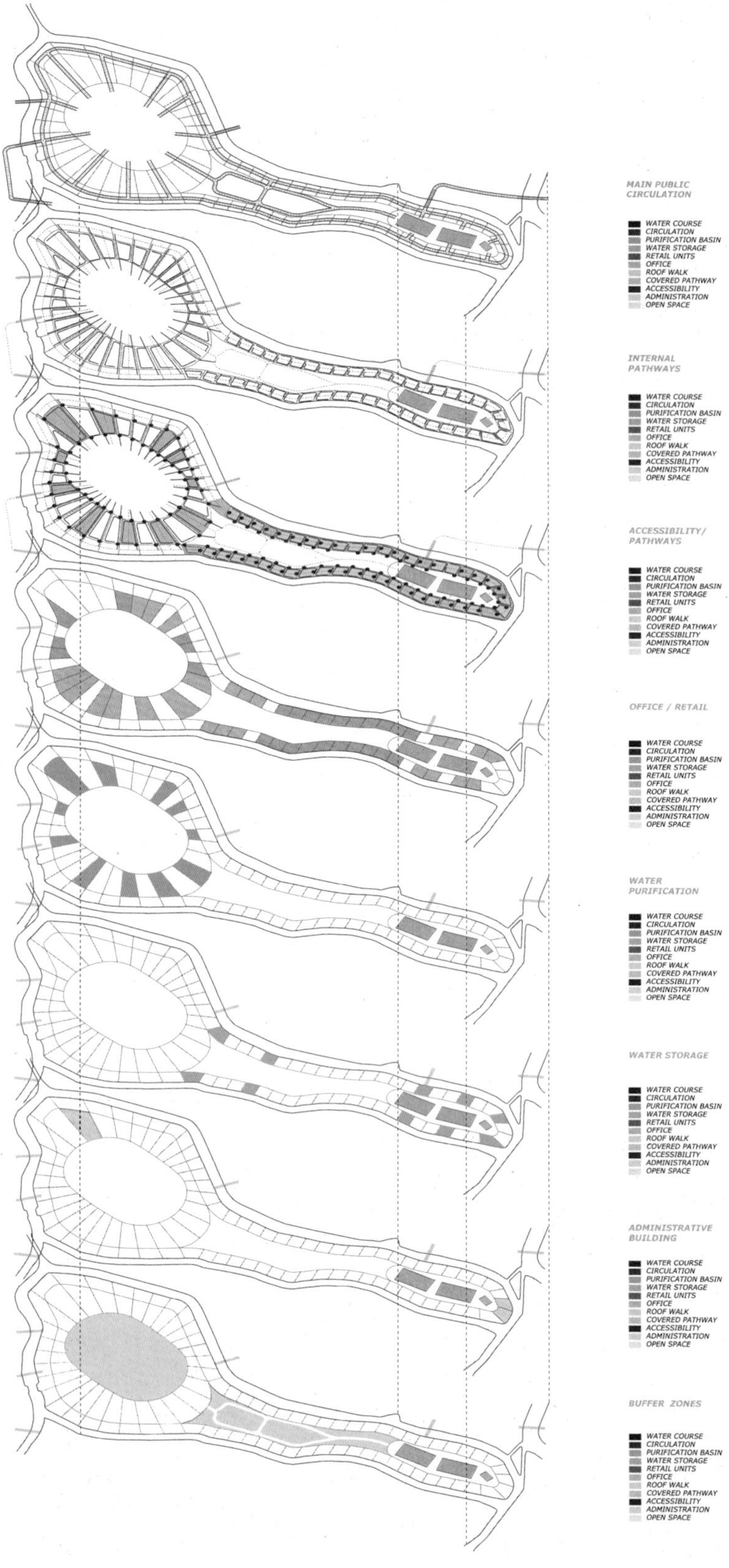

Typical cluster organisation

Legend (repeated for each section):
WATER COURSE
CIRCULATION
PURIFICATION BASIN
WATER STORAGE
RETAIL UNITS
OFFICE
ROOF WALK
COVERED PATHWAY
ACCESSIBILITY
ADMINISTRATION
OPEN SPACE

Section labels (right column): MAIN PUBLIC CIRCULATION, INTERNAL PATHWAYS, ACCESSIBILITY/ PATHWAYS, OFFICE / RETAIL, WATER PURIFICATION, WATER STORAGE, ADMINISTRATIVE BUILDING, BUFFER ZONES

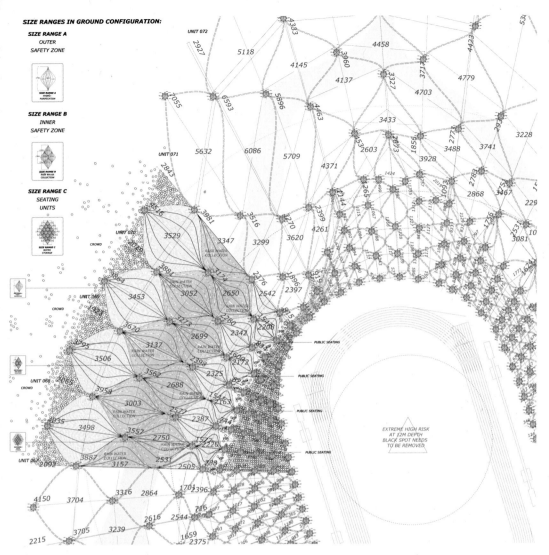

SIZE RANGES IN GROUND CONFIGURATION:

SIZE RANGE A
OUTER
SAFETY ZONE

SIZE RANGE B
INNER
SAFETY ZONE

SIZE RANGE C
SEATING
UNITS

Hydrotype 2012:
articulated fragment plan

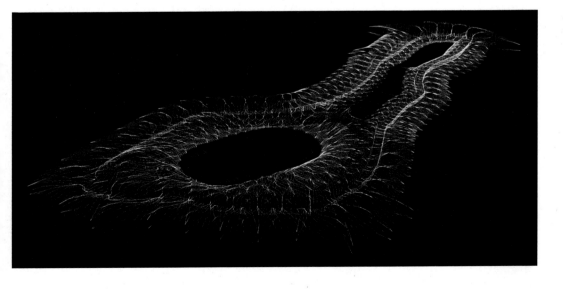

2.2
STRUCTURAL VOIDS
Nankui Lin

Site: Lower Lea Valley, London

Under the current Olympic proposals the Lea Valley will become an inaccessible construction site until 2020, pending the demolition or conversion of the Olympic venues. The scale of structural redundancy – and the waste of investment – seems entirely disproportionate to the duration of the games. Rather than follow this model of phasing, the project proposes a new masterplan that absorbs incremental densities and growth whilst providing for the 2012 Olympics.

The planning is based on a differentiated structural foundation system. The growth of each cluster within the new masterplan is regulated through the installation of two generic column types – the I-Type and V-Type – which may be articulated as low-, mid- or high-rise, depending on the scale of the required Olympic venues and desired building typologies and available investment.

An extensive modelling of the column system revealed its potential to allow typological difference by controlling the distribution of voids and the growth of the structures. In each cluster the strategic organisation of the foundation types regulates specific growth patterns of voids – from distributed to centralised to peripheral groupings – which in turn generates a diverse range of urban fabrics and becomes the mechanism for locating and connecting programmes, from hosting specific Olympic events to the provision of housing and commercial or institutional zones clustered around public spaces.

During the pre-Olympic mode all foundations are laid to conform to the requirements of the sporting events. After this, they are colonised by additional built volumes, in the form of secondary structural elements. Controlling the possible branching or stacking of these volumes through their structural connection points and their load-bearing capacity enforces a fixed void-to-solid ratio, not only on an urban scale but also at the scale of the individual building. This in turn controls diversity within the typologies.

The smooth transitions between the different life-cycles of the development foster continuously evolving building clusters, allowing greater participation within the overall masterplan. Controlled growth through absorption also allows the planning authorities to ensure typological variations or diversity whilst giving greater flexibility to developers and occupants.

Column typologies

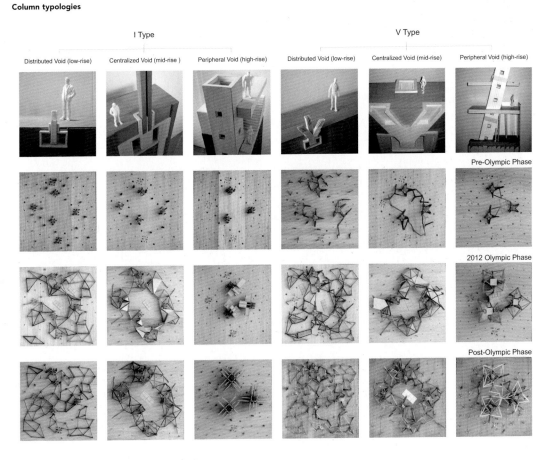

	I Type			V Type		
Distributed Void (low-rise)	Centralized Void (mid-rise)	Peripheral Void (high-rise)	Distributed Void (low-rise)	Centralized Void (mid-rise)	Peripheral Void (high-rise)

Pre-Olympic Phase

2012 Olympic Phase

Post-Olympic Phase

The masterplan is controlled by the planned distribution of different foundation systems that regulate growth within each cluster. The foundations are grouped into two generic families, the I- and V-Column types, whereby the foundation size regulates the implementation of future fixed void-to-built ratios, ranging from low- to mid- to high-rise.

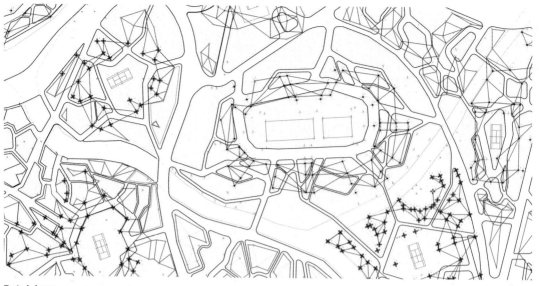

Typical cluster

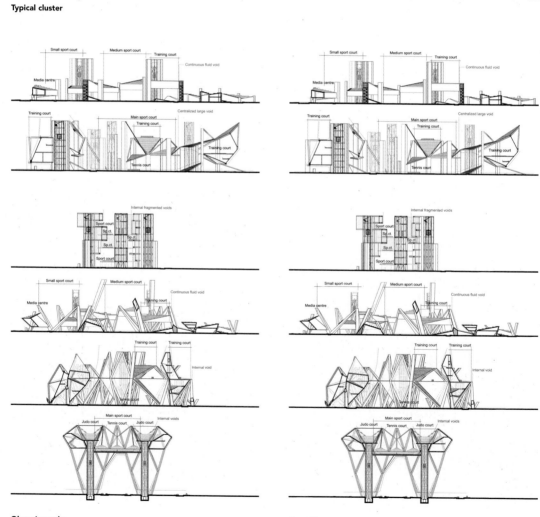

Olympic mode

Post-Olympic conversion/absorption

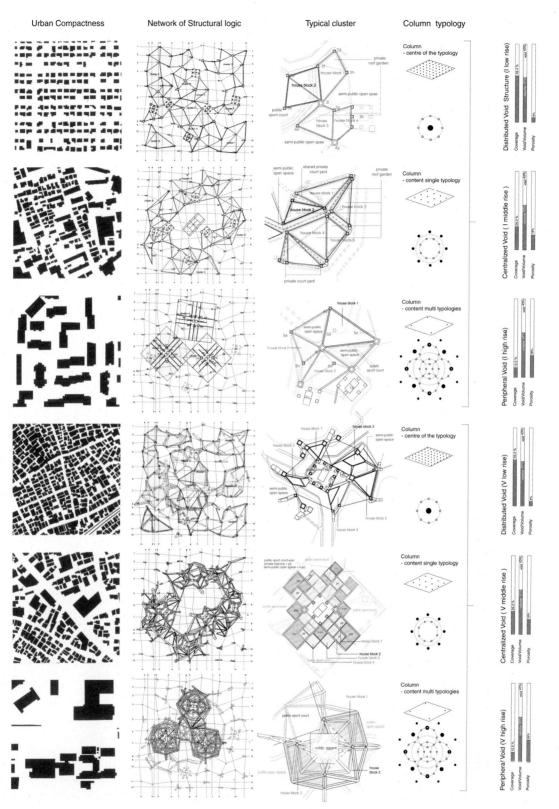

Urban Compactness	Network of Structural logic	Typical cluster	Column typology

I-Column Typologies

In each cluster the strategic organisation of the foundation types regulates specific growth patterns of voids and generates a specific type of urban fabric that enables the hosting of Olympic events, based on volumetric, seating and crowd management requirements. After the games, the primary structural frames are further developed to enable the smooth conversion of Olympic voids into public spaces and the absorption of additional programmes through secondary structural insertions, as required for the legacy phase.

105

I-Column type

Low-rise

High-rise

Pre-Olympic

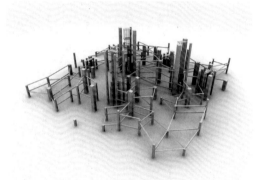

Olympic

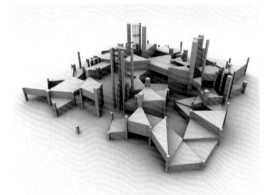

Post-Olympic

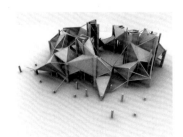

Mid-rise

V-Column type

Pre-Olympic

Olympic

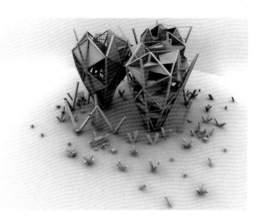

Post-Olympic

Mid-rise

2.3
SPORTS INTERCHANGE
Minseok Kim

Site: Stratford, London

The heavy infrastructure that incapacitates the Lea Valley and prevents its legibility is challenged in this project by means of a sports interchange. A new hybridised infrastructure provides the required sports programmes for the Olympics and utilises the otherwise redundant voids of a 'spaghetti junction'. Building types that usually have destructive urban qualities are combined into a new adaptive typology.

The project proposes an alternative phasing of the site that reduces the period of partial inaccessibility to a mere two years, between completion of the new interchange in 2010 and the insertion of the Olympic facilities in 2012. After the games, the redundant stadiums are transformed into a differentiated public space with facilities and amenities that reinforce the role of Stratford New Town and the larger region as a new recreational and cultural centre.

The Lea Valley Green Belt was created as part of the 1943 Abercrombie Plan. It was intended to check the growth of London to the east, but the relentless expansion of the metropolitan area turned it into a left-over area between east London and Stratford – an industrial wasteland, choked and sliced by high-capacity motorways and elevated railway tracks that make any coherent usage impossible.

The project taps the potential of the Olympic Games to release this frozen land by re-planning and controlling the current infrastructure. Its strategy is to downgrade the infrastructure around the periphery of the Olympic site, and upgrade it around the Stratford area, where major infrastructural works are already underway for Stratford New Town and the Eurostar rail link. The proposed modifications to the infrastructure significantly improve pedestrian and vehicular access to the majority of the Lower Lea Valley by consolidating a new green park and corridor while creating a new primary infrastructural gyratory – the sports interchange – in Stratford.

To maintain ground-level circulation, this interchange takes the form of a spaghetti junction with multi-level connections and distributions. The installation of this hub allows a 'downgrading' of infrastructure elsewhere in the site, which provides a finer-grained circulation system that is more pedestrian-friendly, with better cross-connections.

The ring road is integrated with the stadium through a structural system of slip roads on girders that can accommodate the volumetric programme functions of the games while becoming the seed for a new cultural centre and consolidated park.

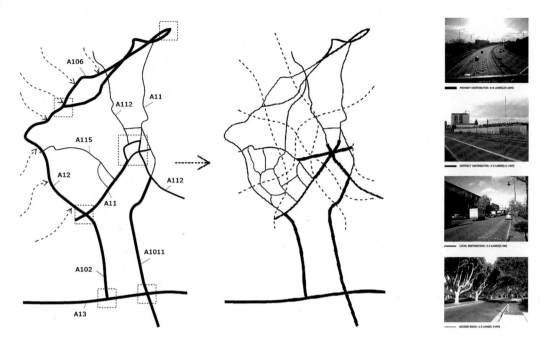

Down- and upgraded infrastructure

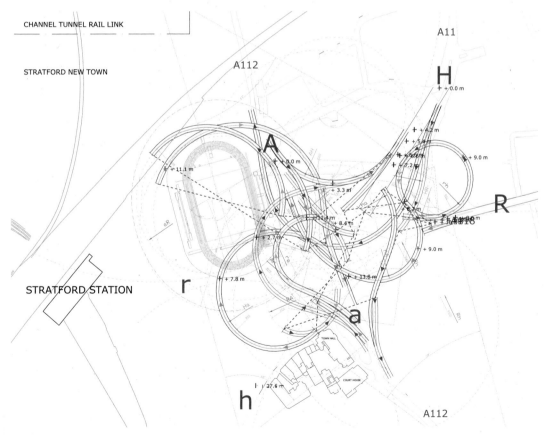

Stratford City: sports interchange

The existing motorways and railway links around the Lower Lea Valley are downgraded into a finer road network that allows local access into the green belt, while the infrastructural hub around Stratford City is upgraded to function as a new sports interchange with several road junctions that redistribute the regional traffic.

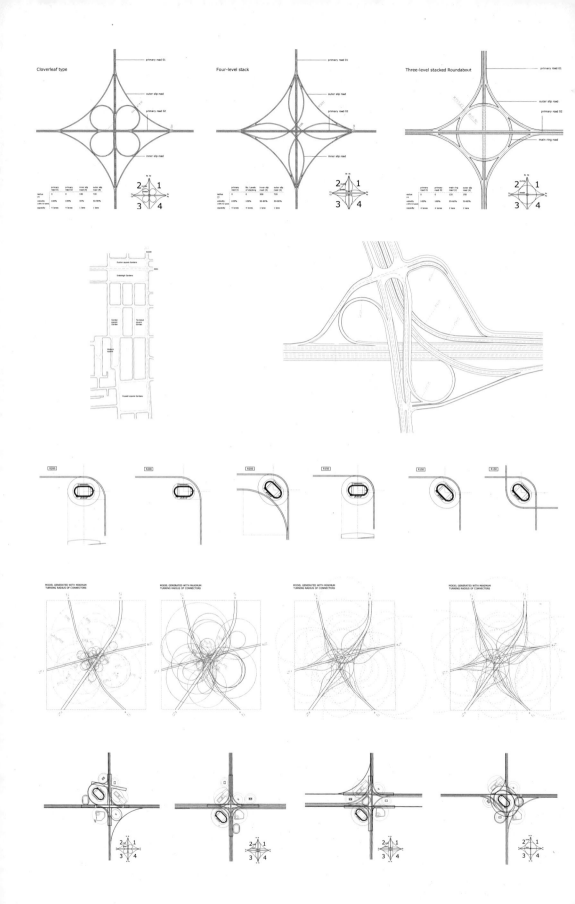

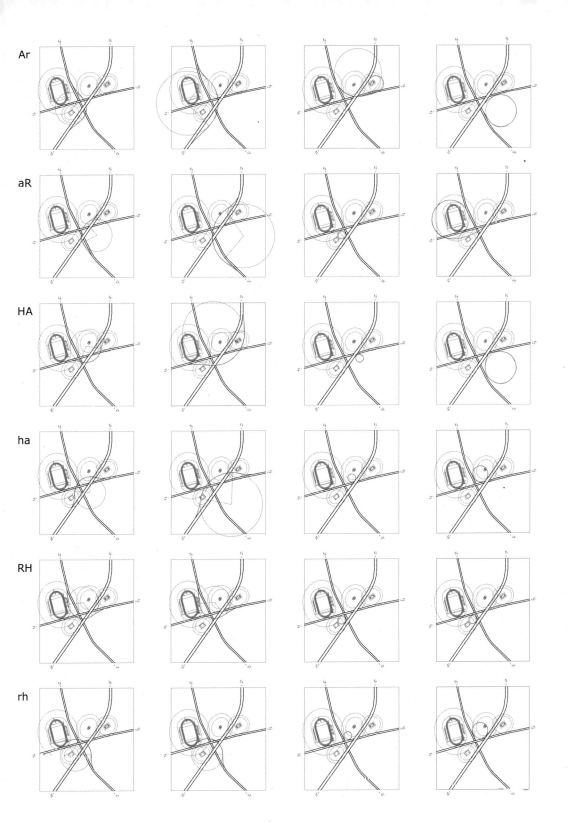

Ar

aR

HA

ha

RH

rh

Study of road junction organisation,
infrastructural fabrics (down- or upgrading) and
outer and inner slip road configurations.

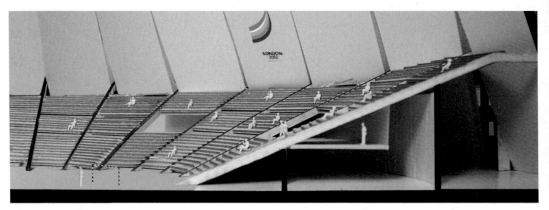

Olympic stadium

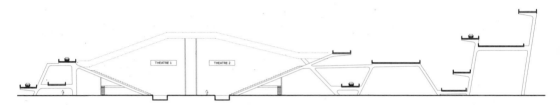

Typical section

Structural frames

Post-Olympic theatre

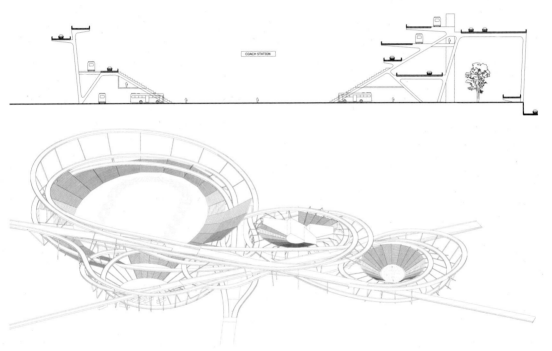

Structural surfaces

The sports infrastructure is constructed as a series of modular frames that support the surfaces of the roads and the seating. The programmatic volumes of support and ancillary functions are inserted into the frames as required by the Olympic masterplan.

The desolate spaces created by the usual spaghetti junctions are utilised as stadiums during the Olympic Games and afterwards are converted into a series of cultural institutions (e.g., theatres) whilst the larger areas become part of the surrounding park.

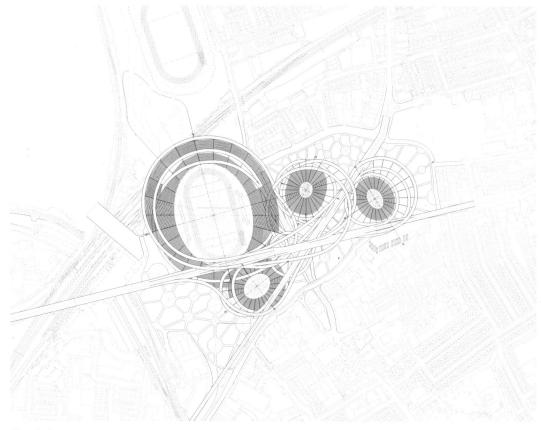

Olympic phase

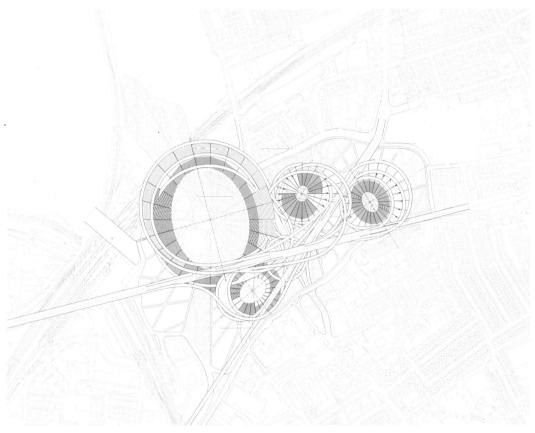

Post-Olympic phase

2.4
MULTIPLE PUBLIC GROUND
Minseok Kim

Site: Convoys Wharf, Thames Gateway

Between 120,000 and 200,000 new housing units are to be built in the Thames Gateway in the near future. In the view of the Environmental Agency and individual insurers, large parts of the proposed development are exposed to a high risk of flooding – yet the design of key sites appears to overlook this danger.

This project argues for new planning strategies that integrate water management and accommodate the emergence of new housing types which respond to the anticipated shift in public ground and the potential for catastrophic flooding. The chosen case study is Convoys Wharf, part of the Thames Gateway. If existing flood defences fail (and it is speculated that the Thames Barrier will become redundant by 2030), Convoys Wharf will disappear, leading to a huge loss of investment and a large-scale displacement of population. Rather than developing a traditional flood-defence system, which would be vulnerable to extreme climatic changes, tidal surges and rainwater run-offs, this proposal integrates three models of water management – storing, channelling and retaining – into a masterplan that enables multiple vertical public areas to be utilised as the water level changes.

The masterplan is driven by the articulation of landforms that are produced via a series of differentiated retaining structures. These function both as the primary circulatory infrastructure and as the foundation system for the buildings, with the overall aim of regulating water management and housing density. A study of fragments of deformed structural grids in the provision of differential housing plots and foundation depths points to an emerging relationship between landform and housing types. This in turn suggests

certain conclusions regarding the effect of multiple ground conditions on privacy and housing types, whilst producing a massing porosity to ensure appropriate environmental behaviour.

Using this fragment performance as a guiding principle, an overall strategic water defence network is dispersed across the site, connecting with the existing public realms and establishing new regulating landforms with integrated housing. Achieved through cut-and-fill, these landforms function as a water-distribution system that reacts to the increase in water levels and activates different vertical layers of the masterplan over time.

Whilst this project used Convoys Wharf as a case study, the strategy could be applied to the whole of the Thames Gateway. Envisioning alternatives that question planning conventions and embrace the potential of these new climatic and ecological conditions, the study suggests adaptive housing typologies that anticipate new lifestyles and respond to changes in social demography and sustainability requirements.

Today

Tomorrow

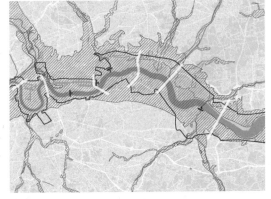

Regional flood map

Local water management plan

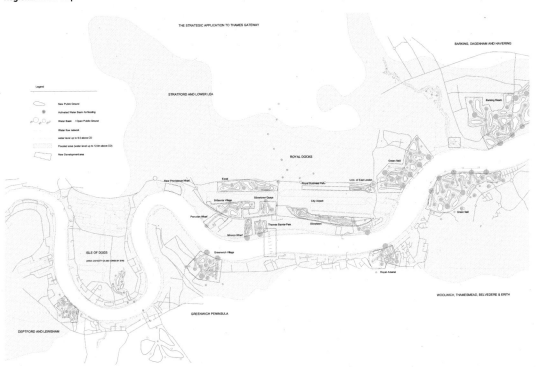

Regional water management plan

As an alternative to traditional systems of flood defence an integrated model is developed that combines water management and land-use, articulating landforms while allowing the partial flooding of development zones.

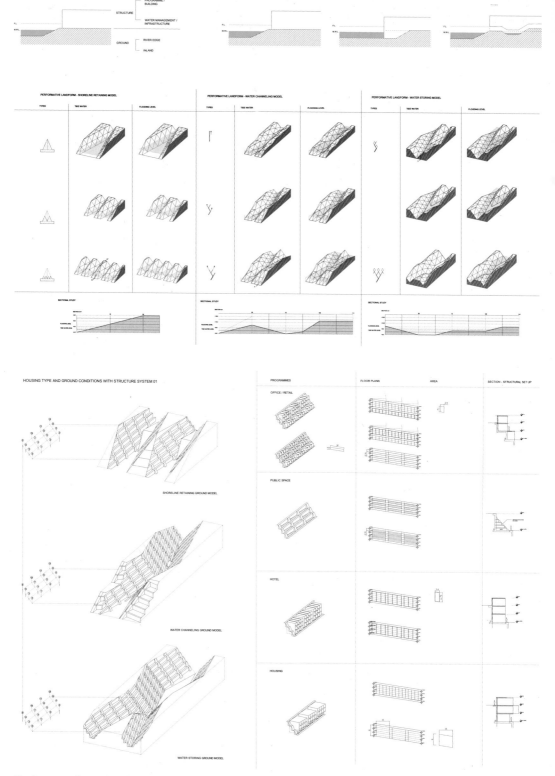

Housing type and ground condition: grid-system 01

Landforms are articulated to fulfil three basic water management criteria: storing, channelling and retaining. They are differentiated through several structural grid-systems that act as retaining structures and foundations, yielding a variety of gradients and plot sizes that determine building typologies and overall housing densities.

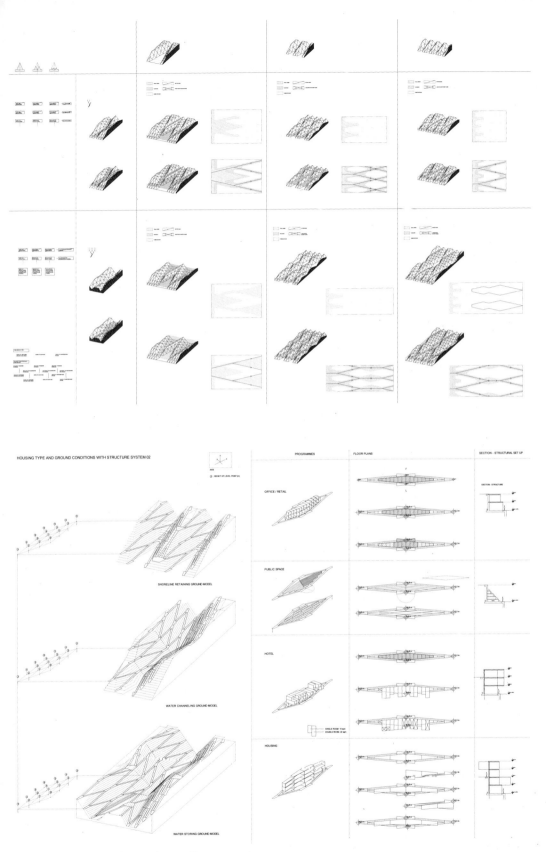

Housing type and ground condition: grid-system 02

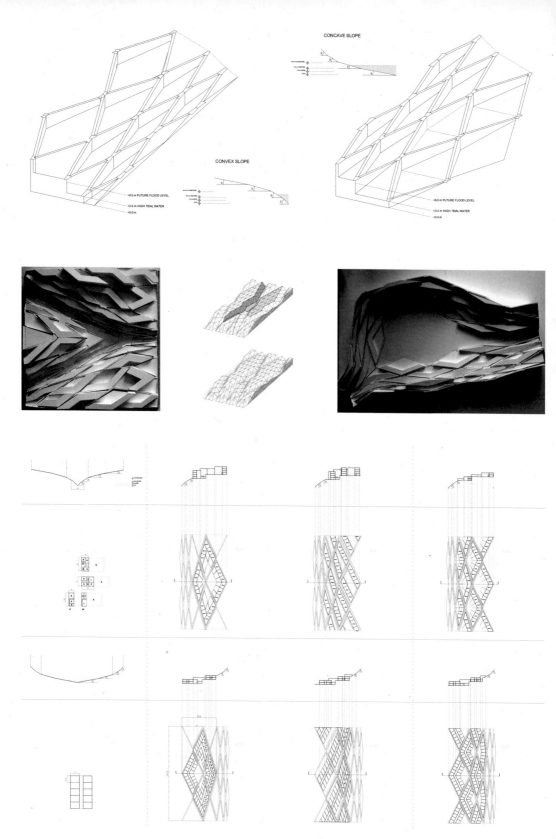

The three performative landforms can be described
through the combination of either concave or convex
sections that are derived through the depression,
summit and ridgeline of each fragment and result in
differentiated fabrics.

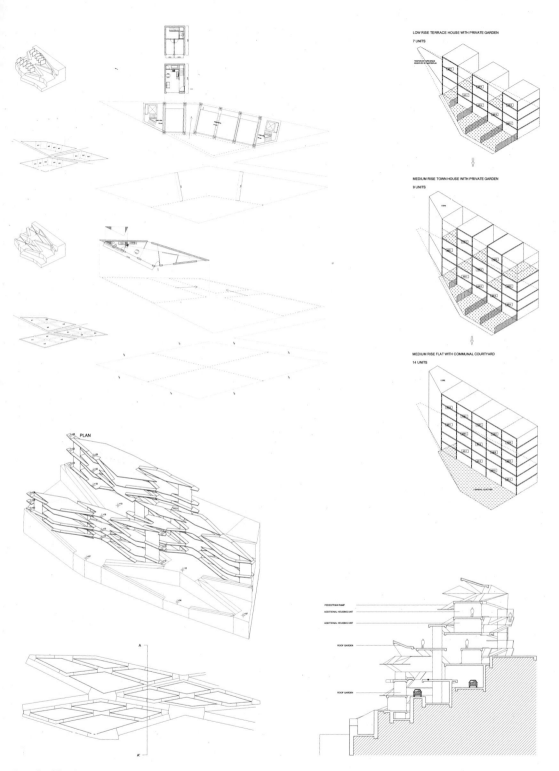

Ground and housing type

The development of each plot, though dependent on the foundation (retaining) system, can be articulated to achieve variations in typologies. Each building accommodates several layers of vertical public or amenity spaces that can be activated when changes in water level occur.

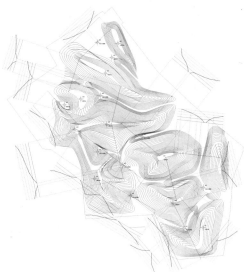

Land formation

Stormwater runoff

Open spaces

Flood response

Circulation system

Housing densities

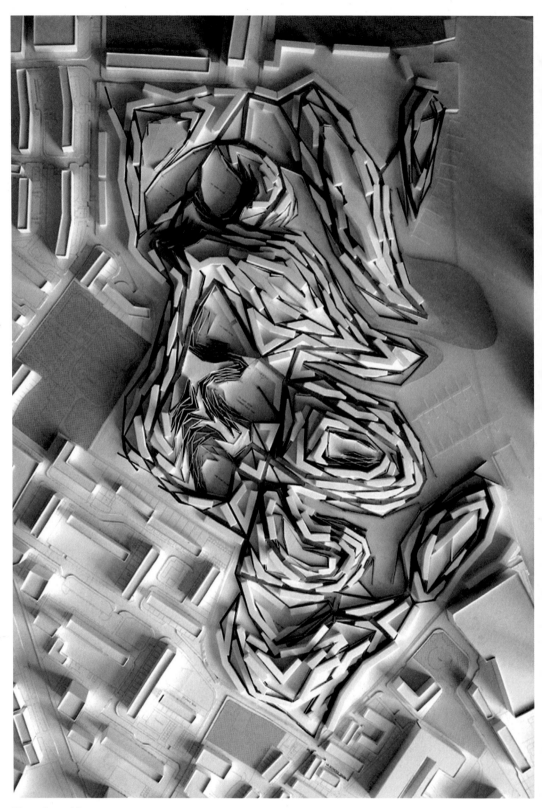

Masterplan model

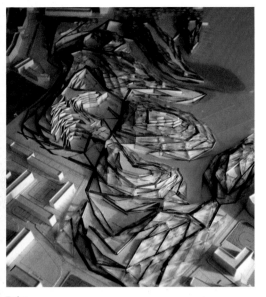

Today

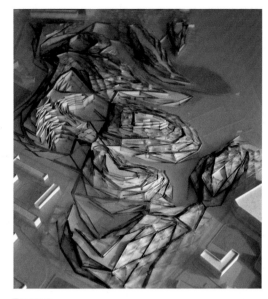

Tomorrow

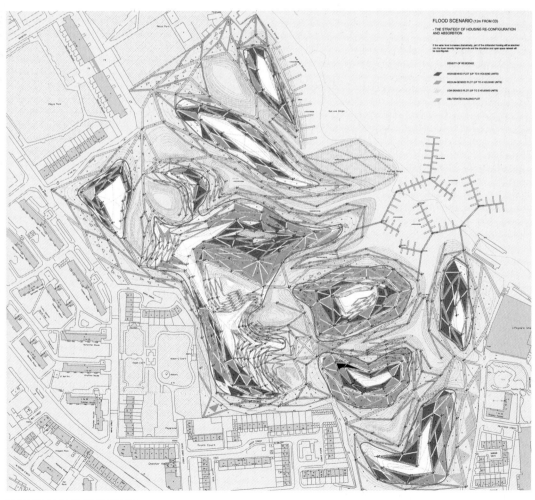

Masterplan: extreme flood scenario

2.5
GAMBLING FOR CULTURE
Charles Peronnin

Site: Cotai Strip, Macau

According to Rem Koolhaas, the Pearl River Delta embodies a mono-programmatic regionalism of exacerbated difference. The urbanism of Macau bears out his analysis: almost 10 per cent of its entire territory is covered by gambling centres. However, this mono-economy is increasingly fragile. The Vegas super-casino model, incorporating mixed-use into the casino footprint, has already failed here, with the Sands Corporation scrapping an expanded cultural programme in favour of yet more gaming areas in what is the world's largest casino.

In this context, the project embraces a mono-programmatic urbanism, offering an armature that is pitched to cluster all of the casino's cultural and conventional facilities into a critical mass of exacerbated difference. Embracing the model of the immersive Vegas-style leisure strip, it speculates on the possibility of seeding an urban potential for growth and diversification which surreptitiously exploits dominant investor strategies to empower local regulatory bodies.

The super-casino frontage, which has evolved in Las Vegas from parking lots to a continuous landscape of thematic enclaves, is now considered as a regulating layer – an exteriorised lobby dissipating the boundaries between public circulation and internal programmes. It is this super-lobby (rather than the super-casino itself) which has the potential to seed a diversification of Macau's leisure economy.

A compression of the interface between public and private developments within Cotai's gambling network is achieved through the vertical segregation of programmatic circulation types whose porosity is regulated by the thematic super-lobby. By activating enclaves (which may be divorced from, or equally merge with, the casino programme) the super-lobby provides Macau with a resilient infrastructure capable of accommodating the failure of temporary mono-programmes.

The vertical circulation of the super-lobby, controlled by its loop clusters (the Las Vegas Strip's *modus operandi*), is articulated via the structural system of a distorted spaceframe. Furthermore, the necessity for a foundation system places the Macanese government in a position to control the growth of the armature, mediating between the gaming operators and those willing to develop the open plots.

The intervention of the government may encourage the Las Vegas Sands Corporation (the sole proprietor of the Cotai Strip) to extend their internal circulation types and provide a framework for the activation and development of flexible and highly differentiated open plots capable of absorbing any expanding cultural programme.

Exacerbated difference

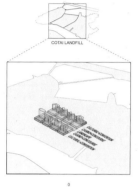

COTAI LANDFILL

ORIGINAL SANDS MASTERPLAN FOR THE COTAI STRIP

0

ORIGINAL SANDS MASTERPLAN FOR THE COTAI STRIP

i.

THE STRIP IS PULLED APART AND EACH SIDE FLIPPED TO FACE THE COAST

ii.

THE LANDSCAPE AND CONCOURSE CIRCULATION TYPES ARE STRETCHED ACROSS THE CENTRAL VOID TO CREATE ARMATURES WHICH CONNECT THE COASTS AND FRAME OPEN SPACES

iii.

THE CHARGED POCHE FABRIC SEEDS THE POTENTIAL FOR FUTURE INDEPENDANT GROWTH OF CULTURAL AND INSTITUTIONAL FACILITIES.

Urban fabric of armatures

ORIGINAL SANDS MASTERPLAN FOR THE COTAI STRIP

THE SANDS MASTERPLAN

THE SANDS MASTERPLAN, LIKE THE VEGAS STRIP, IS LAID OUT ONTO AN INFRASTRUCTURAL ROAD NETWORK WHICH DEFINES RELATIVELY UNIFORM PLOTS

RECONFIGURED COTAI CASINO MASTERPLAN

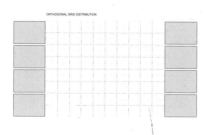

ORTHOGONAL GRID DISTRIBUTION

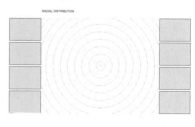

RADIAL DISTRIBUTION

The unbundling of the looped circulation system of the Las Vegas Strip seeds an urban tissue that coagulates as an intensified cultural cluster of exacerbated difference at the centre of Cotai Strip. Such a cluster might survive the expiry of Macau's gambling-driven economy and prompt the creation of stronger cultural institutions.

The loop clusters of the Las Vegas supercasino may be grouped by various means: first, by the differentiation between points and centred open floor clusters; second, by the number and types of satellites composing each cluster, and third, by the number of points shared between the satellites. The grid and armature chosen for the Cotai Strip determine the loop

clusters that can occur within the 'super-lobby' and thus its three-dimensional spatial organisation.

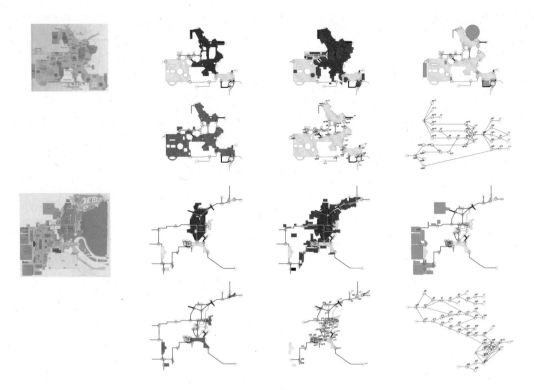

Casino analysis and loop clusters

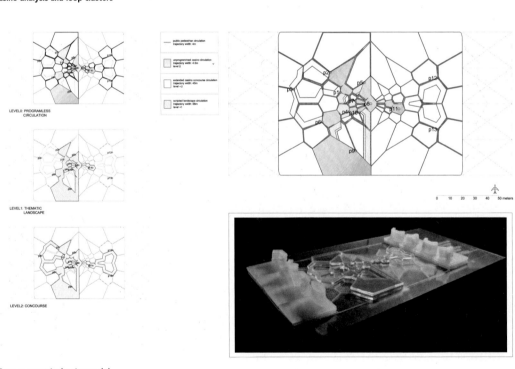

Mono-concentric density model

Supercasinos are characterised by a dense
interiorised urban fabric of intensified
distraction. They are articulated as either
an intricate interweaving of loops or as a
distribution network with critical intersections
enclosed by loop clusters.

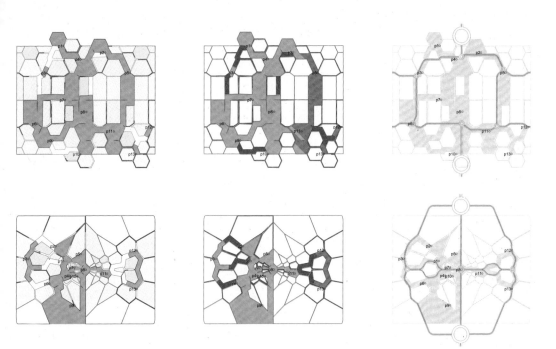

Comparisons of urban armature

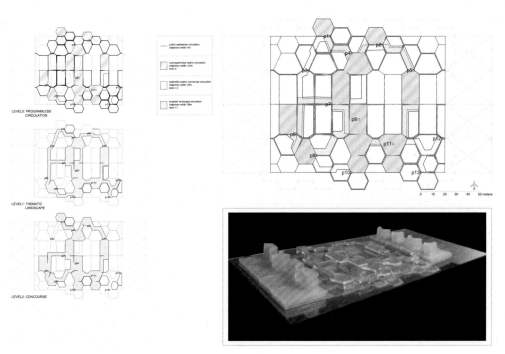

public pedestrian circulation
trajectory width: 4m

unprogrammed casino circulation
trajectory width: 4.5m
level 0

extended casino concourse circulation
trajectory width: 45m
level +2

scripted landscape circulation
trajectory width: 59m
level +1

LEVEL0: PROGRAMLESS
CIRCULATION

LEVEL1: THEMATIC
LANDSCAPE

LEVEL2: CONCOURSE

0 10 20 30 40 50 meters

Variable horizontal strip density model

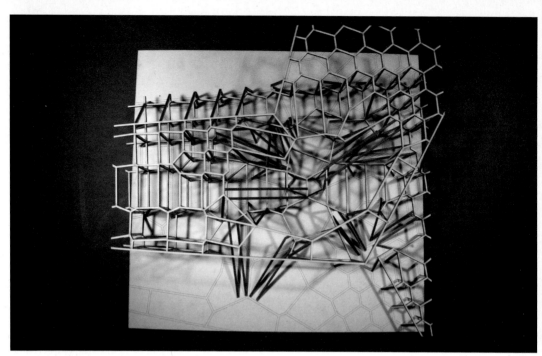

Typical nodal fragment

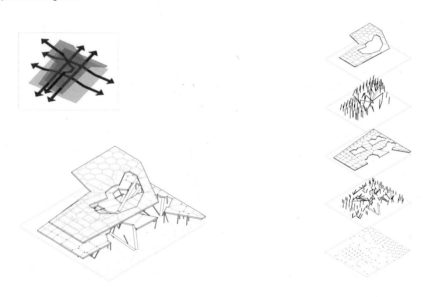

Typical longitudinal section

The Cotai Strip armature is composed of
stacked interlocking and looped circulation
types. The middle landscape level regulates
flows between the continuous public ground
and the top concourse, direct extensions of
the residual casino programme. The landscape
level also administers the varying levels of
porosity on the ground between differentiated
open spaces which can accommodate both
public and private future developments.

Foundation section with piles

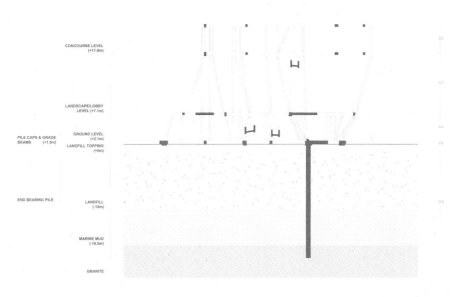

CONCOURSE LEVEL
(+17.8m)

LANDSCAPE/LOBBY
LEVEL (+7.1m)

PILE CAPS & GRADE
BEAMS (+1.5m)

GROUND LEVEL
(+2.1m)

LANDFILL TOPPING
(+0m)

END BEARING PILE

LANDFILL
(-10m)

MARINE MUD
(-16.5m)

GRANITE

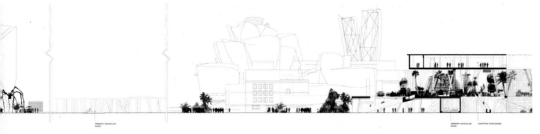

PRIMARY VEHICULAR
ROAD

PRIMARY VEHICULAR
ROAD

EXISTING CONCOURSE

Ground-floor plan

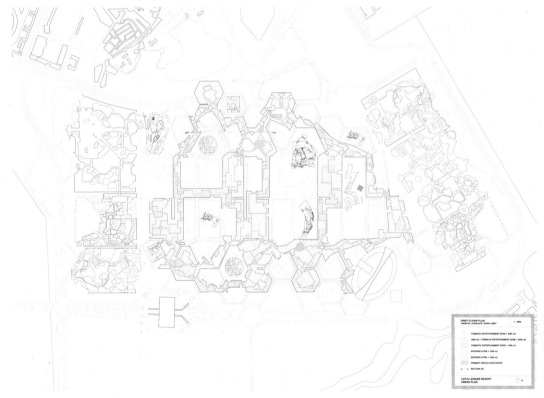

First-floor plan

Roof plan

3.0
TYPOLOGICAL REASONING

Max von Werz, The Projective Arcade

3.1
PROJECTIVE SERIES
Christopher C.M. Lee

> Urban Theory of any kind operates at the level of opinion. It is successful not as a predictive device but as a prescriptive one. Its success is measured to the extent it persuades the undertaking of real action.
>
> William Ellis[1]

Raise the question of type in today's urban context and you risk being branded a historical revivalist or a conservative. Type has not been intensely debated for more than 30 years. Back then, at the demise of modernism, it had become apparent that the generic proliferation of the international style – a prototype born of the union between abstract design and mechanical production – had completely failed to articulate the intricacy and complexity of urbanism and the historical city. A new gospel of type and context in urbanism was promulgated by Colin Rowe and Aldo Rossi, but tragically made flesh in the form of pastel-toned classical revival PoMo architecture by the likes of Rob and Leon Krier, Terry Farrell and Michael Graves.

Substitute 'digital production' for 'mechanical production' and it becomes clear that today's global proliferation of complex forms echoes the conditions of the recent past. A timely moment, then, to reinvoke type? The common understanding of type has become rather stale. For most, it simply means the way in which architects organise their practice profile, classifying work by function – public buildings, residential, commercial, offices and so on. In the context of such stable classifications and groupings, experimentation via type pales in comparison with, say, dabbling in the alchemy of scripting complex forms or geometries.

In and Through Series

Before we attempt to re-establish links between type and the urban plan and stake claims for the renewed relevance of type, it is important to draw out the various conceptions of type and typology. In its most basic sense, type is an object or artefact that belongs to a class or group that brings together others with similar attributes. In architecture, types are most commonly defined by function or genre: schools, offices, hospitals, etc. But types can also be grouped according to shared attributes that are structural, organisational or formal in nature. (For instance, OMA's Y2K House and Casa de Musica are of the same type, despite the disparities in their function and scale.) This is not too different from thinking of the high-rise as a single type, rather than defining it by function as an office tower or residential tower. Typology can therefore be seen as a method of reasoning and experimenting through type – through objects and artefacts considered within a particular group. It begins with precedents and proceeds via variation and differentiation in response to specific but shared demands and pressures. Its aim is to seek new solutions whilst maintaining shared collective traits that are repeatable and have similar characteristics. In this respect precedents, repetition, differentiation and continuity are all crucial to typological reasoning and experimentation.

The idea of type, as part of a more scientific approach to architecture, emerged in the middle of the eighteenth century and found expression in the first taxonomy of building types by Quatremère de Quincy:

> The word type presents less the image of a thing to copy or imitate completely than the idea of an element which ought itself to serve as a rule for the model.[2]

The type and the model should not be confused. For Quatremère, type is an idea – the

1   William Ellis, *Oppositions Reader*, Princeton Architectural Press, 1998, 250.

2   Quatremère de Quincy, 'Type' in *Encyclopédie Méthodique*, vol. 3, trans. Samir Younés, reprinted in *The Historical Dictionary of Architecture of Quatremère de Quincy*, Papadakis Publisher, 2000.

original reason of the thing. The model, on the other hand, is the complete thing. Stressing this difference warns against the biggest pitfall of using type in the production of architecture: namely, that an overreliance on precedents leads to repetition and imitation and rules out originality and invention. Therefore, if the type is an idea, its material manifestation and expression can take on many different forms. Thinking through type allows the architect to reach the essence of the element in question, rather than using it as a model to be copied.

Referring more closely to the model, J.N.L. Durand in the nineteenth century drew up an exhaustive taxonomy in his *Précis of the Lectures on Architecture*. Durand believed that new types would evolve through the recombination of previous types based on compositional rules for reorganising structural grids and axes. The possibility of change inherent in the type gave rise to a structural flexibility that permitted adaptation to the constraints of the site; so the shared and transformable traits of the type could be defined here as the 'deep formal structures' of a building or building types. In the 1970s, Rob Krier saw the taxonomical approach to typology as a means of establishing continuity between new solutions and the historical city. His system was based on the recombination of distilled elements of the historical context. He devised a mix-and-match system based on a small number of distilled elements of the historical city – the square, the triangle and the circle. Although meant as an open system, it was clearly limited and reductive in nature.[3]

The effectiveness of a taxonomical approach largely depends on the manner in which it sets up a process of classification for reproduction. *Phylogenesis: FOA's Ark*,[4] coinciding with Foreign Office Architects' ten-year retrospective exhibition at the ICA in 2004, represents a recent redefinition of the understanding of type. It attempts to construct a consistent and identifiable global practice, not through style or context, but through an analysis of projects seen as a population of material assemblages. This retrospective branding exercise avoids positioning the practice from the standpoint of ideals or critical claims, and instead allows a system of classification to emerge out of an analysis of projects seen as a population. Neatly organised in a 'phylogenetic' family-tree, the practice's projects are classified according to their material manipulations, moving from a two-branched 'function' to a four-branched 'faciality',[5] and so on. As the material manipulations accumulate, species and families emerge, connecting projects across different sites and countries by means of similar traits in organisation and material construction. If one follows the path of this phylogenetic tree, the utility of this taxonomy is evident, in that it serves to both orientate exhibition visitors and help the practice make sense of works in progress. Reading the diagram in reverse allows one to break down a project into its consituent parts – and what can be dismantled can also be reassembled, in more ways than one.

FOA's concept of speciation is instrumental in the sense that it frees the problem of classification from the cages of function, allowing constituent parts of material prototypes to cross-breed and form whole projects. Understanding prototypes as material mediators[6] rather than as function-driven building types allows a greater freedom in differentiating material assemblages: it releases the global architect from the obligation to confront the critical idea of type in a specific cultural, social or political context. According to FOA, the concept of species becomes more relevant as a mediator between a top-down typological design process and a bottom-up parametric design approach. However these taxonomical gymnastics are instrumental only when questions of precedent, repetition, differentiation and continuity – questions underpinning all typological reasoning and design – are internalised within the practice's reservoir of architectural species. There is a vast qualitative difference between the offspring of crossbreeding and the progeny of inbreeding – a difference that cannot be ignored for the sake of internal consistency and clarity.

3   Rob Krier, 'Typological and Morphological
    Elements of the Concept of Urban Space', in
    A. R. Cuthbert (ed.), *Designing Cities: Critical
    Readings in Urban Design*, Blackwell, 2003.
4   Alejandro Zaera-Polo, Farshid Moussavi,
    Phylogenesis: FOA's Ark, Actar & ICA,
    2004, 6–17.

5   ibid., 18.
6   ibid., 12–13.

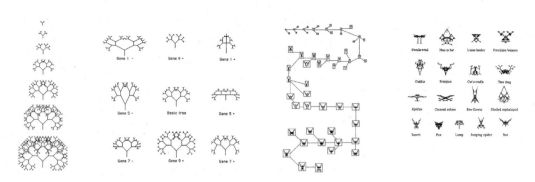

1. Evolution as a non-random process of minor accumulations: growth through branching, nine basic genes and emergence of insect-like figures, from Richard Dawkins, *The Blind Watchmaker*

Suggesting that crossbreeding is preferable to inbreeding is not the same as endorsing the cliché of hybridisation, as a trite response to the desire for difference and multiplicity. The established view – almost an article of architectural faith – is that hybridisation of types via formal manipulations alone will bring programmatic hybridisation under the spell of formal cohesion (usually smooth in appearance). There is an alternative: namely, to allow the hybridisation of the idea and performance of the type by evolving its flexibility and robustness through the precedent via repetition and differentiation.

To draw another parallel with the natural sciences: in *The Blind Watchmaker* Richard Dawkins describes reproduction and evolution as a non-random process of minor accumulations.[7] To illustrate the potential of this process, he wrote a simple program to 'generate' the growth of a tree branch, represented in the form of drawings where one line branches into two, two into four, and so on. The idea was that a few basic reproductive drawing rules would evolve into a variety of tree-like shapes. To further influence this development of cell division or two-way branching, Dawkins created nine basic genes, starting from a single dot and branches, each of varying angles and lengths. Another program was written to reproduce the basic tree shapes by allowing the genes to be passed down from one generation to the next. To Dawkins' astonishment, these shapes did not only evolve into different tree-like shapes but also, after 29 generations of reproduction, insect-like shapes began to emerge, followed later by a whole array of 'insect-figures' (fig. 1). This example offers another way of looking at typology as a productive method for architecture. Although it begins with basic and conventional precedents, the cumulative indexing of genetic imprint is able to produce startling results whilst maintaining continuity, repetition and difference.

As part of the 'London 2013' brief, Kelvin Chu Ka Wing's *'Perforated Hill'* challenges the conventional conception of an Olympic stadium as an architectural artefact impregnated with iconic powers (which fade after a mere 16 days of frantic use and devoted veneration).

These large types are commonly placed on the fringes of the city, surrounded by tarmac and completely closed off from their context. They contribute as much to the urbanity of the surroundings as the average Ikea superstore. The organisation of the stadium is strictly governed by pedestrian escape routes and seating angles. Chu's project takes the inclined escape routes and raked seating as the deep structure of the type, and fixes the capacity of the stadium at 80,000 spectators. It differentiates the type by decreasing the number of routes whilst increasing their overall bifurcation. As the routes branch out and reorganise the spectator seats, the stadium incrementally evolves from a conventional closed bowl into a porous structure. This typological change then opens up further urban possibilities. At the close of the London 2012 games, the stadium can be turned into a

7   Richard Dawkins, *The Blind Watchmaker*,
     Penguin Books, 1991, 43–74.

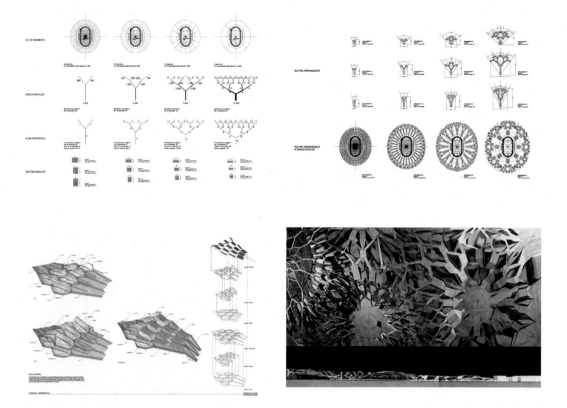

2. Kelvin Chu Ka Wing, Perforated Hill, typological differentiation: stadium type (top left), stadium type as porous structure (top right), volumetric potential towards programmatic seeding (bottom left), layered fabric (bottom right)

perforated hill, with its top layer and the field around it becoming a public park, and the perforated volumes below seeding a fully functional post-Olympic neighbourhood. Overall Chu's project seeks to replace the traditional Olympic Park, dotted with defunct stadiums, with a new city fabric that is able momentarily to absorb the games yet is biased towards the long-term cultivation of a cohesive urban fabric (fig. 2).

These urban strategies are made possible through the differentiation of the type. In order for typology to be a generative design process, it must exploit the potential of an accumulated intelligence of that type, as explored through the diagrammatic imprint of its deep structure. Such a process should allow for the emergence of unforeseen possibilities in the evolution from one type to another, and from type to city – akin to the Dawkins mutation from 'trees' to 'insects' – whilst bearing all the genetic imprint of the parent.

Working typologically therefore means working opportunistically with the generative logic of serial production. It involves both challenging the idea of the type and differentiating its deep structure generatively in response to the initial critical position. Questions of judgement (why the type should change) and power (how it should change) need to be tackled simultaneously. There is no better place to begin this process of reasoning than type's 'natural habitat' – the urban environment, where typological change is directed by the pressures of economic, political and social forces, absorbed, reflected and deflected through the deep structure of the type.

Dominant Types

Understanding, reasoning and then acting upon the urban context typologically should be seen as a means of affecting change at a scale beyond that of the single building. However, as the scale slides upwards, broadening the field of operation, the conflicts between the extent and detail of analysis and proposition increase. The more spatially and architecturally resolved an urban plan, the less receptive it is to change or to alternative visions. Yet an urban plan that is described only in terms of policy and land-use does not offer the spatial and architectural richness or allure that is necessary to shore up consensus and galvanise action on the urban plan.

Repositioning type as a primary element in envisioning an urban plan allows one to draw on its pliability as a constituent part of the urban context and its effectiveness as a medium for channelling the disciplinary knowledge of the architect. Both of these issues hinge on the ability of type to act as an instrument of control, of varying degrees of flexibility. Both Rossi and Rowe argued that an area of study and subsequent intervention within an urban context could be brought into focus either by a sizeable constellation of similar types or by the uniqueness afforded by an architectural artefact. Rossi emphasised historical monuments and housing, Rowe a coherent identifiable pattern of type read in a two-dimensional figure-ground plan alongside historical monuments. This leaning towards historical types (Rossi) or city-pattern (Rowe) was in essence a response to modernism's failure to deal with the historical city and the more nuanced complexities of urbanity. These positions are characteristic of the late 70s; they are also indicative of the common divisions in the discourse around type and the urban context: most critics take the view that you either work typologically or abstractly, are either a contextualist or a modernist, conservative or progressive, specific or generic.

This dichotomous approach belies the simple fact that type is still the dominant force in shaping cities today. The high-rise is now the *de facto* building type of the aspiring global city, exemplified by Shanghai and Dubai. The Burj Dubai Tower is set to become the tallest building in the world, but its final height is being kept a closely guarded secret to preserve the status this will bestow upon the city. The high-rise type (a relic from a previous century) is no longer instrumental on account of its efficient stacking of density or its emancipation of the ground from the building mass. Today, it is its soaring height that is deployed to imbue iconic status and lubricate global PR machines. Another type, the museum, continues to anchor urban regeneration plans, as a landmark and a type largely reserved for and perfected by so-called Starchitects (as in Bilbao, Taichung, Guangzhou and Abu Dhabi), while high-density housing single-handedly dominates many urban plans (including the whole of London's Thames Gateway, for example).

Given the continuing hold of type, the composite influence of dominant types becomes ever more critical in any attempt to stage alternative visions for our cities (fig. 3). Dominant types may still be identified and defined by their potential to effect change, and they can range from collective types that agglomerate to form sizeable fragments or districts, to singular types that are significant either on account of their iconic status, which allows them to act as anchors within their individual urban context, or their proliferation, where the sheer force of numbers substitutes for any discernible quality.

Figure-Ground

Rowe's contribution to the discourse around type and context in urbanism remains invaluable today, for the light it sheds on the problem of using ideal types in an imperfect context (as opposed to the utopianism of modernism's perfectible type). One common criticism of Rowe's contextualism is that the figure-ground plan, rendered as a contrasting

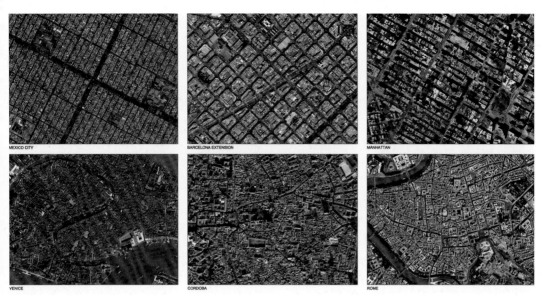

3. Dominant types

solid black vs white pattern of urban fabric (after Nolli's plan of Rome), does not allow for a gradated mix; another is that, regardless of urban context, it conservatively matches new additions with the existing scale and style.

With *Collage City*, the primary ambition of Rowe and Fred Koetter was to mediate between the two inherited images of the city – the traditional city, with its open spaces carved out of solids, and Le Corbusier's utopian *tabula rasa* City in the Park, with its buildings standing isolated on open ground. Using the Nolli plan as a graphic analytical device, they outlined the difference between the traditional city and the modernist city, comparing the figure-ground plan of Parma with Le Corbusier's project for Saint-Dié.[8] The traditional city presents itself as a malleable pattern of urban fabric of a uniform height – type as space-definer. Against this background the urban void becomes the figure, defined by the abutments of uniform buildings and charged as a space of social intercourse through congestion and friction. The city of modern architecture, on the other hand, reveals a fixation with the compositional relationship between objects – an influence carried over from painting, from cubism, purism and suprematism. This preoccupation inevitably favours the object as figure and the void as ground – type as space-marker. The ground plane is wiped clean to make way for the park, in the process destroying the textures and compressive valves that are so vital for spaces of social interaction.

Recognising the dichotomy of the solid-to-void rendering of the Nolli plan, Koetter and Rowe called for a more feathered and filigreed approach to dealing with the edges of the contrasting graphic plan. They offered the poché as a type that allowed for such transitions, being able to engage and be engaged by adjacent voids, and acting as both figure and ground when required.[9] To accuse them of oversight on account of the hard edges of the figure-ground plan therefore seems unjustified. The crucial contribution of Koetter and Rowe to the idea of type in the context of urbanism was to show that pattern-making – through a collaged reading of the figure-ground plan – can be typological. As its title suggests, *Collage City* shows that the abstract pattern can be an incredibly flexible tool for achieving a coherent urban form with defineable voids, mediating the two received images of the city. This approach is abstract but not necessarily generic – and pictorial without being picturesque.

8   Colin Rowe & Fred Koetter, *Collage City*, MIT Press, 1983, 62–3.
9   ibid., 62–79.

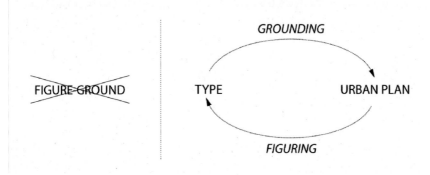

4. Figuring-Grounding

While the figure-ground plan was Rowe's analytical and compositional tool, his source for the making of the pattern was the composite building that was able to effect change by interacting with the urban context. This composite could be either a single structure or a collection of smaller buildings. Working on the large canvas of the urban plan, Rowe inevitably required a rich array of architectural models and resorted to mining historical types for a number of reasons, not least of all because the uniform roof heights of a traditional grouping allowed the 2D figure-ground plan to be deployed more effectively. The sourcing of historical types was also bountiful in face of the problem of filling a blank slate, and acted to resist the image of the city of modern architecture. As a compositional strategy for the large complex building, Rowe used the odd juxtaposition of historical types with a contemporary urban context, seeking to induce a scenic monumental effect through collision and contrast, as opposed to the finer, more resolved composition that results when a coherent group of buildings is used. So the second criticism of Rowe as a conservative, always striving to be 'in keeping', can also be questioned. What Rowe intended was the mutual transformation of the inserted type and the urban context into something altogether new.

However, most of the urban projects that Rowe worked on after *Collage City* reveal that the pattern-making approach of the figure-ground plan resulted largely in urban patterns. The compositional considerations do not in any way challenge the idea of the sampled type or its deep structure, as is evident in the Roma Interrotta project (1978).[10] If type is to be deployed to transform the urban context, it is vital that it undergoes a degree of transformation in order to avoid a typological approach that is both anachronistic and formally deductive.

Figuring-Grounding

For an architectural artefact to have any effect on the urban context, a breach of scale has to be instigated. A crucial means of achieving this is to modify the deep structure of the dominant type in response to the urban context, working towards a reciprocal, cross-scalar co-evolution of type and urban plan. As an alternative to the dichotomy of the figure-ground plan, a more gradated and contingent *figuring-grounding* process appears to promise a typological approach that can engage with the urban context and effect change through the projection of a pliant and reactive urban plan (fig. 4). In this respect, *figuring* describes the process whereby the deep structure of the field (ground) evolves towards a type, breeding and nurturing that type from the conditions of the environment. *Grounding*, conversely, is the process whereby the deep structure of the dominant type (figure) evolves

10 'Roma Interrotta', *Architectural Design*, vol. 49, nos. 3–4, 1979.

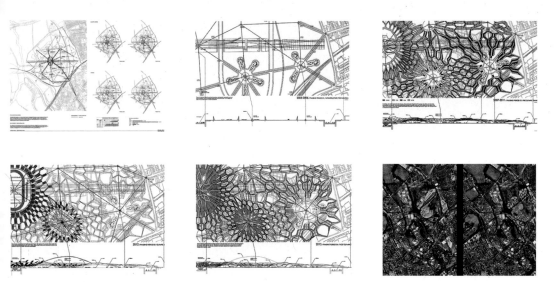

5. Kelvin Chu Ka Wing, Perforated Hill, types as points of growth and phasing of Olympic programmes

towards the field, shaping the structure of the urban plan through the performance of the type. In this way, solid and void become interchangeable and the preference for type as either space-definer or space-marker dissolves. The differentiation of the type attempts to affect the performance of the larger whole – the urban plan – through the control of the elemental part, starting with a precedent type as the most basic component of the urban context. The cumulative indexing of the deep structure of the type enables the transfer of potential from one scale to the other.

This reciprocal evolution of type and urban plan ensures continuity not by matching the style and scale of an insertion to its context, but rather by keeping the genetic trace of the parent or the imprint of the deep structure intact across the various scales of operation. As such, the continuity of the deep structure allows for the prolongation or proliferation of the performance of an intended type in the urban plan, and vice versa.

In Kelvin Chu's project, what started off as the routing system of the stadium type evolved into multi-layered mobility plan that aligns, accumulates and disperses trajectories across the once impermeable stadium and seeds programmatic alternatives into the volumes of the perforated structure. In place of the traditional conception of a sports structure as an independent artefact marooned in a park, Chu's proposal has the stadiums act as a collective form that integrates the current development of Stratford into the Olympic masterplan. The collected programmes evolve through three distinct phases. In the first, pre-Olympic phase, major infrastructural works lay the foundations for a resident population. Next, for the 16 days of the Olympics, temporary seats are installed in the main structures and large voids at ground level are activated to absorb the temporary mass of spectators. Finally, in the post-Olympics phase, the ground is filled in with programmes and the sports fields are transformed into rolling porous hills that merge into the concourse ofthe new Eurostar Interchange and undulate across the Lea Valley, forming a new multi-layered fabric (fig. 5).

The hyper-specific articulation of the type attempts to elude the eventual expiry of the stadium. The project is explicitly described as both a functioning stadium and an urban plan. Here, the urban plan is not described using standard graphic conventions such as land-use colour patches, setback lines or floor area ratios, but is framed in terms of a *typological guideline* that encompasses both scales of performance: the type and the urban plan. Where

6. Marina Bay, Singapore: projection of the state's masterplan and view (top right) of present situation

the conventional urban design guideline favours the uniformity of urban massing and the legibility of the cityscape, the *typological guideline* is more concerned with maintaining the performance of the deep structures of type and the urban plan. It should not be read as a megastructure designed to be implemented as a total piece of architecture, but rather as a set of instructions that specifies a typological performance in an urban plan.

Degrees of Freedom

A highly differentiated and articulated urban plan of this kind quite easily arouses suspicions of totalitarianism in relation to both its ambition and its outcome: it is commonly assumed to be inflexible, to offer only a singular vision, excluding difference. By contrast, a less resolved urban plan is thought to impose a reduced level of control, creating more opportunities for future developments to flourish. According to this logic, an urban plan described solely by a generic equal grid of infrastructure allows the most freedom, with the natural outcome of such unbridled freedom being diversity, in the form of inclusive

144

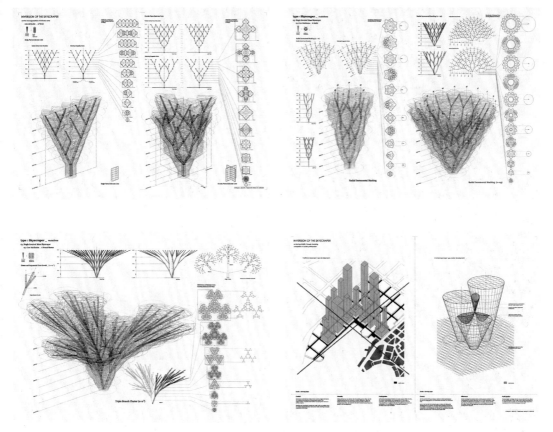

7. Yicheng Pan, Resisting the Generic Empire, typological differentiation in inverted high-rise: planar (top left), radial (top right), clustered (bottom left), shared public volume (bottom right)

participation. But one need only look at Sheikh Zayed Road in Dubai or Pudong in Shanghai to realise that an equal distribution of plots nourished by gridded motorways offers an extremely limited kind of freedom. Large corporations and developers are left to pursue their singular visions. The plots spawn no other type but the high-rise and the ground plane is selfishly hogged by opulent, hermetic hotels and sleek corporate lobbies. Individuals or groups without direct access to vast amounts of capital are disqualified from any form of ownership or direct participation. Such developments are the apotheosis of the freedom so favoured and exploited by global capitalism.

Exploring these issues of control and difference, Yicheng Pan's 'Resisting the Generic Empire' challenges Singapore's addiction to the ubiquitous high-rise type and confronts the state's inability to conceive of any new development that is not populated by high-rises. Marina Bay is a 139-hectare reclaimed site originally earmarked for development under the state's ambitious 1996 masterplan, but the 1997 Asian economic recession left it barren for over a decade. Recently, under a new leadership, the state has decided to reapply the failed masterplan, this time repackaged with iconic structures that promise to deliver a plane of spectacular skyscrapers (fig. 6). Yet a masterplan that is homogeneously structured for the mass production of these high-rise structures increases the city's dependence on the precarious global market. It takes away its ability to respond quickly to change, as each plot can only be developed through massive economic investment.

To wrest control of the ground plane from the endlessly proliferating skyscrapers,

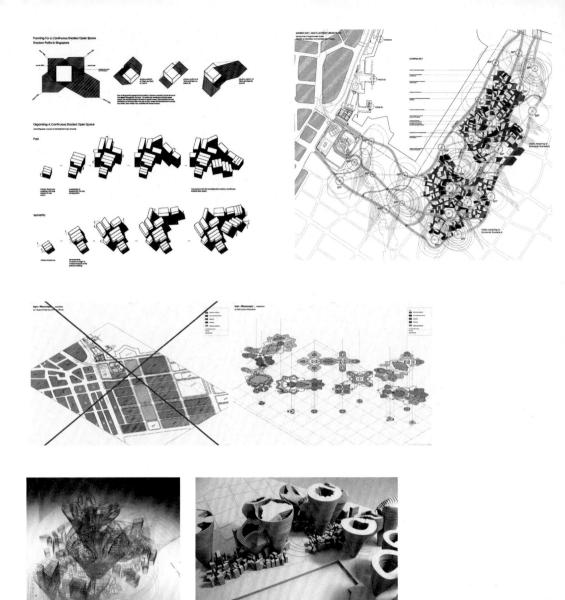

8. Yicheng Pan, Resisting the Generic Empire, ground fabric growth to provide shaded spaces (top left), multi-layered urban plan (top right), inverted high-rise and revalorised ground plane (centre), layered topological guideline (bottom)

Pan inverts the skyscraper's massing through the cultivation of multiple urban plans within the skyscraper type (fig. 7). This strategy not only releases the ground plane for immediate activation by smaller building types but also creates multiple 'clustered' volumes for increased public and private partnerships. The project, in this way, resists the formation of the state-engineered Generic Empire – a city entirely subjugated to the whims of large corporations – by providing a typological framework that cultivates difference through the coexistence of multiple types. The released ground place is further articulated with a fabric that creates a continuous surface of shaded open spaces suited to the tropical climate and to occupation by smaller and more diverse stake-holders (fig. 8). For Pan, the best way to promote difference and participation in a city-state like Singapore is not to relinquish control but rather to intensify it, forcing a typological change that encourages the participation of the wider population.

The projects by Chu and Pan use the potential of a differentiated type that is subsequently deployed in an urban plan. Both are regulated through a *typological guideline* that creates a diversity in plot sizes and configurations, more varied public and private volumes, overlays of mobility plans and a gradated hierarchy of public spaces. An explicit rejection of the one-size-fits-all generic urban plan, this approach assumes that for diversity to flourish, a framework indexed with a wide range of possibilities must be in place to absorb a more varied constituency of stake-holders and galvanise consensus for action.

Thus to work typologically is also to work in a series, harnessing the cumulative intelligence of the type in question and surpassing both its idea and its deep structure. In order to induce typological change, the idea of the type needs to be critically confronted. A systemic approach is required to differentiate the type's deep structure so that it surpasses its precedent whilst maintaining its genetic imprint. Working typologically in the urban context therefore requires a recognition of the potential and relevance of dominant types as a collective urban entity with the potential to seed, differentiate, regulate and administer the urban plan. Typological reasoning and production are complementary, critical and generative at the same time; both have the potential to valorise and politicise the urban plan by shifting from the neutral ground occupied by a disinterested architectural artefact towards a charged ground that is contested or negotiated – a ground that can be more closely understood as land to be defended, trespassed on or claimed, a ground that sustains an ideology through type, with the architect as a projective type-maker.

BIBLIOGRAPHY

Giulio Carlo Argan, 'On the Typology of Architecture', reprinted in Nesbitt, Kate (ed.), *Theorizing a New Agenda for Architecture: An Anthology of Architectural Theory 1965–1995*, Princeton Architectural Press, 1996, 242–6

Alan Colquhoun, 'Typology and Design Method', in *Theorizing Architecture*, op. cit., 250–7

Richard Dawkins, *The Blind Watchmaker: Why the Evidence of Evolution Reveals a Universe Without Design*, Penguin, 1991

K. Michael Hays (ed.), *Oppositions Reader*, Princeton Architectural Press, 1998

Jeffrey Kipnis, 'Performance Anxiety', in *2G: Foreign Office Architects*, Nexus, 2000

Jeffrey Kipnis, 'Re-originating Diagrams', in *Peter Eisenman: Feints*, Skira, 2006

Rob Krier, 'Typological and Morphological Elements of the Concept of Urban Space', in Cuthbert, A.R. (ed.), *Designing Cities: Critical Readings in Urban Design*, Blackwell, 2003

Rafael Moneo, 'On Typology', in *Rafael Moneo 1967–2004*, El Croquis, 2004

Aldo Rossi, 'An Analogical Architecture', in *Theorizing Architecture,* op. cit., 348–52

Aldo Rossi, *The Architecture of the City*, MIT Press, 1984

Colin Rowe & Fred Koetter, *Collage City*, MIT Press, 1983

Aleajandro Zaera-Polo, Farshid Moussavi, *Phylogenesis: FOA's Ark*, Actar/ICA, 2004

3.2
WHAT'S YOUR TYPE?

Sam Jacoby

> … typology presents itself as the study of types of elements that cannot be further reduced, elements of a city as well as of an architecture… no type can be identified with only one form, even if all architectural forms are reducible to types. The process of reduction is a necessary, logical operation, and it is impossible to talk about problems of form without this presupposition. In this sense, all architectural theories are also theories of typology, and in an actual design it is difficult to distinguish the two moments.
>
> Aldo Rossi, The Architecture of the City, 1966

By 2030 it is anticipated that 60 per cent of the world's population will be living in urbanised areas. Questions surrounding the development of our cities are therefore taking on an ever greater urgency, with designers increasingly forced to address the escalating politicisation of architecture through its relationship with urbanism. The nature of this relationship is traditionally polarised between the dual figures of architect and masterplanner, each exploring proposals at very different scales. The resulting lack of coherence and inability to incorporate the diversity of requirements defines the majority of contemporary city planning, so that any hoped for synthesis between architecture and urbanism remains lost.

It is the potential of this union between the urban and the architectural that lies at the heart of our work, with our students challenged to look critically at a number of current development plans in London and other European and Asia cities. All of these plans share a date of anticipated expiry following a performance defined by its sense of spectacle and branding, brought to the fore through one-off events like the 2012 Olympic Games or via mono-programmatic planning, as in the case of Europe's largest shopping centre, currently under construction in London's White City. Being dependent on specific events, businesses and industries, these plans are liable to become obsolete once their original use ceases to provide the necessary critical mass. This inherent problem is exacerbated by a reliance on icons and superlatives provided by a familiar coterie of name architects, each carefully chosen to deliver structures that advertise an established architectural brand yet are as susceptible to obsolescence (through their generic repetition) as the plans that they celebrate.

Our alternative approach is one based on the concept of type, chosen in particular because of its ability to synthesise content and form and operate at the scale of both the building and the city. One recurring focus was on organisation and the concepts of control, difference and flexibility within a masterplan, and their effect on specific building types. A rethinking of these critical aspects of organisation allowed us to define structures that we termed *dominant types*, as they create sufficient critical mass within a given masterplan to provide an instrumental platform for understanding the urban through a series of architectural interventions. The process of defining these complex relationships and their impact on the formation of the plan could be further described as a process of *typological reasoning*. However, this reasoning is not primarily a formal endeavour, but demands an understanding of the broader political and economic context, situating specific architectural problems within a masterplan while setting the parameters for further typological investigations. Neither is this strategy a covert attempt to repackage the idea of *genius loci* or historicism; rather, it seeks the formulation of relevant strategies for effective policy-making, dealing with questions of form and content within a multi-scalar masterplan reactive to contemporary concerns.

In order to detail the precise nature of this typological reasoning, one needs first to revisit and overcome the burden of its historical baggage. What, after all, is the status and function of type in architecture? And how can type be more than a static field of self-referential confirmation, solely dependent on pre-taxonomised figures and precedents and solidified in a classification system exemplified by Neufert's ubiquitous *Architects' Data* (an approach that has resulted in its widespread rejection as a basis for any serious intellectual effort)?

Almost since the birth of type in architecture there have been two distinct doctrines on type, each with its own devout followers. One – epitomised by Marc-Antoine Laugier's 'primitive hut' (1753) – bases concepts of type on idealistic or primitive models (archetypes) that refer to the imitation of nature and propagate a generic formal content. The other derives type from a practice-driven design methodology that pursues a differentiated solution of specific formal instances (prototypes). Generally these doctrines are seen to be diametrically opposed – a view reinforced by Anthony Vidler in his influential text 'The Third Typology', which defined three historical phases in the conceptual appropriation of type: the Enlightenment, the Modern Movement and Neo-Rationalism.[1] Departing from Vidler's view, I would suggest another historiography of type – a reading that acknowledges the continual co-existence of the formal and cultural aspects of type. On the one hand, I would propose a lineage from Quatremère de Quincy to Aldo Rossi and Rem Koolhaas, as proponents of a culturally driven concept of type, where architecture is understood as a language-like process with a critical content. On the other hand, there is the tradition from Jean-Nicolas-Louis Durand to Le Corbusier and Peter Eisenman, where typal ideas are pursued as a means to derive new forms and organisations as a product of a generative process.

All architctural histories of type – regardless of the ability of historians to establish types of type – essentially begin in 1825 with Antoine-Chrysostome Quatremère de Quincy, who was the first to systematically introduce the notion of type into architecture. In his *Encyclopédie Méthodique,* he outlined a general aesthetic system based on elementary principles defining the epistemological roots of knowledge and origins of architecture. Bounded by a concern with aesthetics, an important part of his theory is the transferral of type from the fine arts to architecture, with a critical distinction made between *type* and *model*, or imitation and copy, with the former suggesting a higher and ideal order and the latter functioning as a utilitarian device.[2]

In the mid-eighteenth century Laugier had located the origin of architectural forms in the unified 'primitive hut', which simultaneously embodied an abstract concept of materiality and a construction dependent on the signification of nature through imitation. By contrast, Quatremère's dual conceptualisation makes a clear distinction between a metaphysical theory

1   Vidler suggests three distinct concepts of type. The first one is associated with the period of the Enlightenment, when an ontological understanding of nature gave rise to the idea of type defined by Quatremère de Quincy and Durand. Later, the modern movement, aligned with the rational sciences, formulated an analogy of technological production implying a 'quasi-Darwinian law of selection'. Finally, the neo-Rationalists, advocating an 'ontology of the city', defined the 'traditional city as the locus of [their] concern' and referred to the continuity of form and history embedded in the public and political nature of all architecture. While the transformation of selected types was their primary concern, they achieved this not through a rigorous transformative process, but through a strategy of metaphoric opposition. Anthony Vidler, 'The Third Typology' in *Oppositions 7*, MIT Press, 1976.

2   'The type presents less the image of a thing to copy or imitate completely, than the idea of an element which must itself serve as a rule for the model... The model, understood in the sense of practical execution, is an object that should be repeated as it is; contrariwise, the type is

an object after which each artist can conceive works that bear no resemblance to each other. All is precise and given when it comes to the model, while all is more or less vague when it comes to the type. Concomitantly, we see that there is nothing in the imitation of types that sensibility and the mind cannot recognize, and nothing that cannot be contested by prejudice and ignorance.'
Quatremère de Quincy, 'Type' in *Encyclopédie Méthodique*, vol. 3, trans. Samir Younés, reprinted in *The Historical Dictionary of Architecture of Quatremère de Quincy*, Papadakis Publisher, 2000, 254–5.

3   'Imagining no other imitation than the one whose model is obvious to the eye, they fail to recognise all the degrees of moral imitation; that is, the imitation of analogy, by intellectual relationships, by application of principles, by the appropriation of manners, combinations, reasons, systems, etc.'
ibid., 255.

and a scientific or practical approach. The model, nevertheless, is not to be misinterpreted as an exact copy, but is constituted by *formal resemblance*, a reproduction of kind, whereas type is a product of *moral imitation*,[3] a cultural and intellectual effort. Considering architecture as a social institution similar to the structure of language, the *Encyclopédie* entry on 'type' describes how social and cultural context condition formal differences, an idea developed from his earlier writing, *De l'architecture egyptienne*.[4] Rather than using function to define type, Quatremère argues that variations in type are engendered by the effects of socialisation and the methods of construction indigenous to each culture.[5] Thus, unwilling to be constrained by Laugier's singular vision of origins, Quatremère expands the archetype of the hut into a tripartite entity, now including the primitive *tent* and *cave*. Incorporating the specificities of culture and society, his proposed idea of type implies a profoundly speculative, inventive and epigenetic process, not tied to a particular style but universally relevant.[6]

The relevance of Quatremère's notion of type to architecture – as both a vehicle of historical understanding and a means of establishing a design methodology – was reconsidered by the neo-rationalists in the 1960s, following their rebuttal of architectural modernism and its perceived urbanistic failures. Inspired by Giulio Carlo Argan's article 'On the Typology of Architecture',[7] they revisited the history of architectural forms. The most famous of these revisionist histories was Aldo Rossi's *The Architecture of the City* (1966), which proposed an alternative *rational* method to analyse the formation of the city through the study of its history and its *urban artefacts*, identified as those spatial structures that transform over time. Fundamental to this method was Quatremère's idea of type as a cultural and historical product that has the potential for a typological process independent of a generative functional system. Rossi also follows Quatremère's belief that architecture is a formal expression of its society through typological manifestations, analogous to the transformative structure of language.[8]

Through Rossi, the city becomes explicitly synonymous with architecture, assuming the role of its collective consciousness. Its constituents are read as primary elements: housing, fixed activities, circulation and, in particular, urban artefacts as monuments – or elements of *permanence*. In other words, the deep structure of the urban artefact is that of the architecture of the city, with its associated history and typology. This integral relationship is embedded further into the concept of *permanences*, which in tandem with Rossi's notion of memory counters the modernist dependence on functionalism to understand the city, noting that

4 Winning the Prix Caylus for this essay in 1785 launched Quatremère's academic career. A revised version of the essay was published under the title *De l'architecture egyptienne considérée dans son origine, ses principes et son goût, et comparée sous les memes rapports à l'architecture grecque*, Paris, 1803.

5 'There is more than one path that leads back to the original principle and to the formative type in the architecture of different countries... Thus, once that kind of combination, to which the use of wood is susceptible, is adopted in each country, and – depending on the demands of construction – becomes a type that is perpetuated by custom, perfected by taste and accredited by immemorial usage, it ultimately passes into enterprises in stone.' Quatremère de Quincy, *Encyclopédie*, op. cit., 255.

6 For more details on Quatremère's concept of type as an epigenetic process, see Sylvia Lavin in *Quatremère de Quincy and the Invention of a Modern Language of Architecture*, 1992, 86–100.

7 Argan differentiates between an ideal type, imitative in quality, and a generic type that is 'never formulated a priori but always deduced from a series of instances,' defining type or root form as 'the interior structure of a form or as a principle which contains the possibility of infinite formal variation and further structural modifications of the "type" itself'. He also argues that the use of the model implies a value judgement and acceptance of past solutions, whereas typological reasoning stimulates a critical and creative process that synthesises precedents with formal invention, by merging the discourse of typology with that of tectonics. This, he claims, enables the resolution of formal definitions, addressing problems beyond those of function and structure alone. Giulio Carlo Argan, 'On the Typology of Architecture', in *Architectural Design*, no. 33, 1963.

8 'I would define the concept of type as something that is permanent and complex, a logical principle that is prior to form and that constitutes it... Ultimately, we can say that type is the very idea of architecture, that which is closest to its essence. In spite of changes, it has always imposed itself on the 'feelings and reason' as the principle of architecture and of the city.' Aldo Rossi, *The Architecture of the City*, trans. Diane Ghirardo and Joan Ockman, MIT Press, 1984, 40–1.

functions change over time. To comprehend the artefact, it is necessary not only to consider its generic function or form but also, more importantly, its individuality and the continuity of its form, which persists even after the original use ceases. This change demarcates a turning point, when the artefact converts from an object of history to a subject of collective memory. Through permanence, architecture also obtains formal and functional autonomy and begins to condition urban transformations. Typology's independence from function is further secured by its simultaneous existence as both the *analytical moment* of architecture and the means of instituting new (typological) realities – a dichotomous role achieved by conflating type-form with its *locus*, the specific place of 'memory and collective nature of singularity', where the individual history of an artefact finds both its expression and formation.

To recognise emerging type-organisations, a new classification system for buildings is suggested, one based not on function but rather on a consideration of the effects of urban geography, formal, economic and historical influences as manifestations of the cultural and social context. However, Rossi's analogy-based theory of the city can only be comprehended as a comparative and historical mechanism that depends on the assumption that the city is a temporal and man-made object, with spatial continuities materialising in its primary elements and architecture. These elements 'have the power to retard or to accelerate the urban process' and their 'dominant formal and spatial characteristics' make up the city. Hence the diversity of the historical city can be understood through a study of a characteristic areas, or more specifically a vertical slice (*recinto*), which embodies its complex formation.

By placing urban development under the control of 'principal artefacts' or 'primary elements', Rossi challenges the established mechanisms of urban planning and privileges the architectural scale, giving it regulating and administering powers.[9] The accompanying transition in scale, from architecture to urbanism, is possible, as according to Rossi, no qualitative changes to urban artefacts occur during this process of modification. This in turn, however, raises the crucial question as to how one composes these principal artefacts. Rossi suggests that they are 'produced by technical or artistic formation', as architectural design is an autonomous process, an amalgamation of economic and social demands, profoundly contributing to the realisation of architecture as a social institution and forming an 'analogous city'.[10]

One answer to Rossi's dilemma of form can be found in Rem Koolhaas's work, which exploits the diagram as a means of directly conceiving type-forms. First, he problematises accepted type-norms by questioning their diagrams of programme distribution and organisation. These diagrams are then reorganised according to a process of cultural reasoning or a narrative logic, resulting in their literal translation into form. Thus, in the Seattle Library, the traditional library type is redefined as an 'information store'. The proliferation of digital and virtual media is acknowledged and finds expression in its spatial structure and layout. Reflecting on its changed programmatic functions and social status, the renewal of type becomes a product of an already existing cultural condition. Its form is plausible, as it remains an autonomous yet consequential product of the dialectic between form and function negotiated by the diagram.

Following this line of a cultural reading of the role of type, the first brief given to our students during the year could be described as strategic in nature, understanding architecture as a response to political, social and economic realities. This work owes a debt to Quatremère's notion of type conditioning formal differences through its link to a cultural

9 ibid., 96: 'Of course, we cannot so easily entrust the values of today's cities to the natural successions of artifacts. Nothing guarantees an effective continuity. It is important to know the mechanism of transformation and above all to establish how we can act in this situation – not, I believe, through the total control of this process of change in urban artifacts, but through the control of the principal artifacts emerging in a certain period. Here the question of scale, and of the scale of intervention, comes to the fore.'

10 ibid., 116: 'Architecture, along with composition, is both contingent upon and determinative of the constitution of urban artifacts, especially at those times when it is capable of synthesizing the whole civil and political scope of an epoch, when it is highly rational, comprehensive and transmissible – in other words, when it can be seen as a style. It is at these times that the possibility of transmission is implicit, a transmission that is capable of rendering a style universal.'

context, as well as to Rossi's *analytical moment,* a conflation of architecture and urbanism into type. Our other point of departure is type's fundamental autonomy from function and its performance as an indexical device of history and form as demonstrated in Rossi's concept of collective memory and permanence.

The first question we need to ask about type concerns its potential to synthesise and facilitate urban conditions and production. Problematically, Rossi locates the origin of all urban synthesis in the unattainable social concept of the Greek *polis,* the *mental place* of the democratic city-state that is both a real and an ideal place of *nature.*[11] The mythological relationship of the city and its citizens with nature is meant to overcome the inconsistency that exists in his argument between the city as an autonomous construct of a collective will on the one hand and the demands or desires of individuals on the other. But Rossi's text never makes it clear how the artefacts of the city can resist individuals and transform into the collective consciousness without regressing to a fake historicism or collage, as implied in his analogous city.

If, by contrast, the conception of form is located in present cultural milieus, the individuality and singularity of the object does not necessarily prevent its transformation into the collective, but instead enables it – as can be seen in the work of Rem Koolhaas. In this work the diagram is used as an instrument of transposition, as it carries no formal allegiances, unlike the traditional form-dependent taxonomies of types.

The contradictory relations between content, form, society, culture and history also inform the typological reasoning within our projects. First, based on an analysis of issues such as redundancy, control and flexibility, or ecology and sustainability, we identify a series of dominant types that are specific to their site and cultural context. In contrast to Rossi's urban artefacts, these dominant types are not dependent on historical continuity but are instead defined by their potential to enact a new urban plan through performative consistency. The dominant types are analysed in relation to each other and within the larger context of their infrastructure. They are also measured against the usual parameters of urban design, such as mobility, density, land-use, open space distribution and phasing, etc. This analysis is complemented by a diagrammatic study of the history of the dominant types aimed at distilling their organisational and performative in/stability and understanding their potential to react to outside forces of redundancy and expiry and effect change.

The resulting projects, following the initial location of typological conflicts, can be described as working either through the figure or through the ground (*figuring* or *grounding*). But whereas the Nolli plan of Rome or Colin Rowe's understanding of the gestalt figure-ground relation are based on singular plan-based distribution of public and private space, the projects developed a series of layered plans or sections that define the urban plan as a three-dimensional differentiated set of relations resisting simple extrusion. Some projects started with an enquiry into particular dominant types and their potential to directly affect the constitution of an urban plan. Others dealt with the potential of the ground as infrastructure to locate specific typologies within a masterplan, while another series of projects rethought the value of the icon, using it as a performative rather than a discrete object of branding to create long-term development potentials and benefits.

This first brief, therefore, is about formulating a critical thesis that develops a typological conflict and strategy, identifying dominant types within a specific urban site through the study of its planning parameters and cultural context, framing the potential of a typological reading of the urban plan. The subsequent second brief, however, takes these dominant types and explores them as a set of generic type-forms or type-organisations in order to evaluate the performative effects of differentiation and proliferation at scales that range from the architectural to the urban. This approach is akin to another tradition of type

11   ibid., 136: '[T]he Greek city did not have any
     sacred limits; it was a place and a nation, the
     abode of the citizens and thus of their activities.
     At its origin was not the will of a sovereign but
     a relationship with nature which took the form
     of a myth.'

as a formal or generative instrument, and through an accompanying focus on ideas developed by Durand and Le Corbusier, among others, the resulting work explores the constructs of model and prototype.

Writing around the same time as Quatremère, Durand did not himself use the term type, but preferred *genre* to denote buildings with different functions. However, he relied on the underlying idea of type to devise a scientific approach to systematise architectural knowledge through classification. In the *Précis of the Lectures on Architecture* (1802-05), written as an introduction to architecture for engineering students at the École Polytechnique, Durand divides architecture into two classes, public and private buildings. These are further subdivided according to their function and features in terms of structure, material, form and proportions. This comprehensive taxonomy becomes the basis for a set of instructions on how to design new compositions combining these *elements*, first by creating the various parts of the building, such as porches or stairs, and then relating these parts to each other and to the building as a whole.[12]

To reinforce this unprecedented position of architectural production as a formally autonomous and scientific process, Durand denies the effects of style, proposing geometric abstraction as an alternative source of structural organisation. Based on the duplication and subdivision of *building elements* within a rigorous grid and along axes, this technique could be applied equally to the whole city, or just to parts of it. For Durand, buildings were elements of the city, in the same way that building elements were the constituent parts of a building. Another radical aspect of Durand's work is its rejection of established concepts of origin and imitation, as endorsed by Vitruvius and Laugier.[13] He declares the desire for completeness, beauty and pleasure to be obsolete, subsumed already in *utility*, the demand that architecture satisfy our needs through *fitness* (*solidity*, *salubrity* and *commodity*) and *economy* (*symmetry*, *regularity* and *simplicity*).

Many echoes of the rationalist instructions of Durand's *Précis* may be found in Le Corbusier's doctrine, for all its denunciation of history. *Towards a New Architecture*, published in 1923, has a thematically similar structure to the *Précis*. Le Corbusier states his belief in architecture as a fulfilment of utility – as Durand had done some 120 years earlier. However, fitness and economy now carry connotations of a new mass-produced modern life-style; they no longer refer exclusively to the actual construction of buildings. Le Corbusier also reverses the conception of harmony embodied in utility, reintroducing aesthetics as the explicit principal objective of architecture and referring back to classical proportional systems and orders, as is well illustrated in his later books on the *Modulor*.[14]

While Le Corbusier defines architecture as a *plastic thing*, he still shares with Durand the conviction that a viable design methodology must use pure geometries and platonic solids, organised and distributed by axes or *regulating lines*, in order to generate new formal arrangements. Geometric abstraction remains a necessary part of the process of generating new formal arrangements, but is kept separate from the actual production of architecture.

---

12 'Having thus established general principles in the introduction, we have given an account of the elements of buildings in part I: engaged and detached supports, walls and the openings in them, foundations, floorings, vaults, roofs, terraces, and so on. These features have been considered with reference to the materials from which they may be constructed and to the forms and proportions that they may assume. In part II we have shown how these elements may be combined together, both horizontally and vertically; how to form these combinations into the various parts of the building, namely, porticoes, porches, vestibules, stairs both external and internal, rooms, courtyards, grottoes, fountains, and so on; and, finally, how to combine the parts: that is, to dispose them in relation to each other and to the composition of a building as a whole.' J.N.L. Durand, *Précis des leçons d'architecture données à l'École Royale Polytechnique*, trans.

David Britt, Getty Research Institute, 2000, 74. A similar description is also given in *Précis*, vol. 2, 132.

13 He vehemently asserts, that '[t]he order, as objects of imitation, have nothing to contribute, because they resemble nothing in nature.' ibid., 88.

14 'Architecture has another meaning and other ends to pursue than showing construction and responding to needs (and by "need" I mean utility, comfort and practical arrangement). ARCHITECTURE is the art above all other which achieves a state of platonic grandeur, mathematical orders, speculation, the perception of the harmony which lies in emotional relationships. This is the AIM of architecture.' Le Corbusier, *Towards a New Architecture*, trans. Frederick Etchells, Architectural Press, 1946 edition, 102–03. Originally published as *Vers une architecture*, Les éditions G. Crès, 1923.

The plan becomes the rational generator, creating perceived spatial performative effects by modulating the three-dimensional masses and surfaces, as outlined in his *Three Reminders* to architects.[15]

Notwithstanding these similarities, a significant difference occurs in relation to the idea of type. Durand's type is a taxonomical device, whereas Le Corbusier uses synergies of multiple typological effects to regulate building as a *'system of functions'*. Function now is understood dynamically and the relation between structure, function and spatial organisation is no longer a given.[16]

This radical departure from the modernist axiom of 'form follows function' informs a subsequent preoccupation with typological synergies, epitomised by his architectural prototypes from *Maison Citrohan* to *Immeubles Villas* and the *Cartesian Skyscraper*. Yet these prototypes, and his celebrated manifesto *Five Points of Architecture*, only came into being through the initial invention of an archetype – the *Dom-Ino*. By separating function from structure, this opened up the possibility of the *plan libre*, testing the limits of traditional genre-based typologies.[17]

The autonomy of form and function is taken further by Peter Eisenman, who substitutes questions of type with investigations into a formal language driven by the use of the diagram and the concept of *architecture's interiority*.[18] There is an explicit interest in the diagram as a means of formally exploring questions of *presence*, the role of the *sign in architecture* and the relationship to *desiring subjects*. These concepts are directly related to Rossi's notions of sign and event, permanences, singularity and individual or collective consciousness,[19] but in opposition to Rossi, Eisenman's theory pursues architecture's formal autonomy without recourse to historical models. The diagram is now a device through which the limits of architectural form can be explored. As seemingly unforeseeable spatial and organisational differences are revealed, a variety of new typological possibilities emerge.[20] For example, the *Church for the Year 2000* challenges the traditional cultural and material order of the church, proposing a new liturgy and organisation. In Eisenman's work, the *diagram of anteriority* not only embodies the accumulated history of architecture, but also directly establishes organisation and form within its process, while preventing classification through traditional taxonomies.

The typological development within the second brief attempts to establish strategically driven prototypes with clear performative values, derived from dominant types. Formal variations or differentiations within this framework are investigated by a process

15 'For the architect we have written our 'THREE REMINDERS.'
MASS which is the element by which our senses perceive and measure and are most fully affected.
SURFACE which is the envelope of the mass and which can diminish or enlarge the sensation the latter gives us.
PLAN which is the generator both of mass and surface and is that by which the whole is irrevocably fixed.
Then, still for the architect, "REGULATING LINES" showing by these one of the means by which architecture achieves that tangible form of mathematics which gives us such a grateful perception of order.'
ibid., 21–2.

16 See also Bruno Reichlin, 'Type and Tradition of the Modern' in *Casabella*, 509/510, January–February 1985.

17 Ironically, and despite its novel appearance, the product of the *plan libre* (such Villa Garches, built in 1927), shares the comparative formal and organisational principles of Villa Malcontenta, a Renaissance precedent by Palladio, as has been pertinently observed by Colin Rowe in *The Mathematics of the Ideal Villa and Other Essays*, 1976.

18 Peter Eisenman, as editor of the English translation of *The Architecture of the City*, has written about Rossi's work and through *Oppositions* has been involved in the publication of many other articles related to the question of type.

19 'The problem with this idea of the diagram as matter, as flows and forces, is that it is indifferent to the relationship between the diagram and architecture's interiority, and in particular to three conditions unique to architecture: (1) architecture's compliance with the metaphysics of presence; (2) the already motivated condition of the sign in architecture, and (3) the necessary relationship of architecture to a desiring subject.'
Peter Eisenman, *Diagram Diaries*, Thames & Hudson, 1999, 30.

20 ibid., 35: 'The diagram acts as an agency which focuses the relationship between an authorial subject, an architectural object, and a receiving subject; it is the strata that exist between them.'

of analytical drawing through abstracted diagrams. The diagrams become an important instrument with which to experiment with the efficacy of type and understand its formal limits. Being reduced to a singular solution, type becomes a means of testing possibilities.

This organisational investigation also considers how individual types function as a collective cluster within an urban plan, creating the critical mass to affect its constitution. The projects have looked at planning parameters of specific types, such as structure, circulation, programme distribution, massing, access to natural light and viewing angles, as well as (and especially) the interface where ground and building meet (e.g. foundation systems, podium designs) and models of integrated infrastructure. The typological differentiation then takes place within these planning parameters, taking account also of the 'cultural' reading of type from the first brief. For example, how does the distribution of differentiated column systems affect the massing, programme distribution, density and organisation of types through its control over voids? Or how does a perforated or lop-sided stadium-type allow the consolidation of specific urban edge conditions, or the intensification of nodes? As types are organised three-dimensionally, their efficacy cannot be fully investigated at the level of a singular plan, but instead requires sectional differentiation and control. Thus the plan-based axial or mono-programmatic zoning dominant in Durand's or Le Corbusier's urban planning is effectively challenged with the building up of a three-dimensional and multi-layered relationship between type and urban plan.

From the ideas of type discussed above, it is apparent that typology is a discursive field of knowledge, formed of multiple, evolving interpretations. The use of type, typology, prototype, archetype, model and diagram encompasses reflections on programme, function, form and morphology. More significantly, it involves the expression of a specific ideological and cultural agenda informing a design methodology.

This work, then, is not exclusively concerned with techniques of diagramming, hybridisation, topological studies, networks, protocols, etc., but is an attempt to define a broader approach to typology that recognises its capacity to respond to singular and individual forms and demands while determining shared organisational characteristics that allow for an effective negotiation with the external or internal forces present in any urban context. This effect can be traced, for example, in the series of projects that directly tackled the iconic shaping of the stadium typology, transforming it into collective forms that accommodate within their structural organisation the infrastructure, housing and businesses promised by the Olympic Legacy Plan. By making the clustered typology subservient to regeneration requirements, a new urban plan and reality is envisioned that addresses redundancy through typological integration. Rather than resorting to historical precedents, these projects use indexical diagrams to analyse the innate requirements and organisation of stadiums. Some of the projects also attempt to reinterpret the potential of building types as connective fabrics that are indexical of their surroundings, as a way of establishing an effective relationship between the urban and the architectural plan through type.

The final brief, *Projecting the Urban Plan*, is concerned with the synthesis of architecture and urbanism. It applies the earlier typological reasoning to the realities of a specific urban site, negotiating the generic with the specific. One recurring issue is that of administering and regulating the urban plan through control and flexibility, or the role of participation and ownership. This raises the question of generic organisation, approached through a synthesis of programme, structure and volume, and relies on an analytical drawing process to disclose and problematise typological questions, with the aim of allowing a vital preliminary evaluation of the speculated *adaptive typologies*. To assist the necessary translation between scales of organisation, the conclusions are further formulated as typological guidelines, whereby the typically singular masterplan is described as a process of incremental growth characterised by a dominant building type. Finally, a proposal based within a strategic fragment of the studied site explores not only its causal, functional or structural production but also its spatial and material performative effects as a work of 'real' architecture.

Some projects, for example, reject the icon as a lazy urban design tool and develop alternatives that strategise the effects and function of phasing. The singular masterplan vision is undermined through typological invention that responds to the cultural context and allows an increase of control, public activity and flexibility of investment and zoning, along with greater levels of participation and functional difference. Other projects looked at the potential of (infra-)structurally driven plans to directly affect the design and organisation of building typologies. Here, phasing is superseded by the absorption and conversion of additional built volume within the superstructure over time. Without the need for a large-scale demolition or overhauling of the infrastructure, this produces typological variation and continuous change of building clusters. Thus regeneration does not depend so much on instant large-scale investment by the government, but is facilitated by controlled difference and incremental growth, with development incentives allowing investors to gain density in return for providing long-term investment in public facilities. In other projects, the potential of ecological conditions informed new housing typologies that not only take advantage of the increase in value and desirability attached to waterfront properties, but also envision direct planning policies for sustainable design, synchronising the phasing of the masterplan with the decontamination or colonisation of the land. In this way, the projects begin to redefine typology as a field of knowledge through which planning and architectural issues can be rethought and suggest direct operative and instrumental possibilities.

Ultimately the approach of the unit attempts to reconcile the complexities of the urban condition defined by rapid cultural change with a radical new understanding of architecture's autonomy. Rather than pursuing continuity, our typological reasoning enables a consistency that is less a formal and more an organisational idea affecting the urban plan and architecture. Thus our work is also an attempt to reflect on the very purpose of conducting architectural research, not solely as a hermetic or pragmatic production, but as a means of promoting typologically reasoned invention and synthesis.

3.3
THE COMPLICATION OF TYPE

Lawrence Barth

Architecture and urbanism are being mentioned in the same breath with encouraging regularity these days. Both in practice and in teaching programmes, urbanism seems to have become a natural complement of architecture and an important domain of its critical application. Of course, some see the union in completely unproblematic terms – imagining the urban simply as a continuation of architecture on an extended scale. The fact that there is a close and intricate relationship with architecture is an important starting point, but describing this as continuity on a terrain of quantity or extension is very much open to question. Urbanism does not belong to architecture in that sense. The tendency to see the relationship in such a way may be something of an unfortunate hangover from the 1960s thinking that brought typology and the city together in a critique of modernism. A more encouraging aspect of the coupling resides in the natural synergy between the experimental impulse of architecture and the strategic demands of urbanism. On the occasion of just such an experimental exploration of typology and the urban plan conducted in the AA's Diploma Unit 6, we might review the conceptual legacy which has formed the backdrop to their innovations.

We might begin by returning to the question of the continuity between architecture and urbanism which was so central to the last period of enthusiasm for typological exploration in the 1960s and 1970s. By the time Rafael Moneo was reviewing that literature and its associated practice in 1978, there was a pervasive critical impulse to define the city in all its structured richness as the site of the modern movement's failure. Among many who aimed to remedy architecture's standing in relation to urban growth and culture, he could point to Saverio Muratori, whose work in the 1960s helped to initiate a revisionist approach to architecture and urbanism that would emphasise historical and structural continuity between the two. For him, 'the idea of type as a formal structure demonstrated a continuity among the different scales of the city... These types were seen as the generators of the city and implicit in them were the elements that defined all other scales.'[1] These larger-scale typological elements were the streets and voids that wove themselves into patterns of integration and differentiation among types and across scales. While types were understood as active generators of the city, we might also notice that they were constrained to produce the image of the city. Typological description and classification found itself provisionally subordinated to the urban plan, registered through a particular set of visual materials that emphasised figure-ground studies and perspective drawings of iconic urban spaces. Architecture and the urban could be linked via a consistent visual imagery translated smoothly across scales.

For some, this particular configuration of typological and urban reasoning was something of an event in architectural urbanism. Anthony Vidler famously marked it out as the Third Typology, and described the important ways in which it differed thematically from both the early modernists and the eighteenth-century rationalists.[2] Thirty years on, it appears to have done more to clarify points of dispute than initiate a new consensus. In hindsight, it did little to shift the basic lineaments of the discursive formation linking architecture and urbanism, and little to freshen project-driven design research. If anything, it probably provided a new codification and justification for an existing conservative tendency, in the literal sense, within the urban process. But few within architecture seem to have been satisfied with an urbanism of small things and minor variations; in fact, the urban process

1   Rafael Moneo, 'On Typology', *Oppositions*, 13 1978, 35.
2   Anthony Vidler, 'The Third Typology' in Kate Nesbitt (ed.), *Theorizing a New Agenda*

for Architecture: An Anthology of Architectural Theory 1965–1995, Princeton Architectural Press, 1996, 260–3.

itself seems to have become dramatically unleashed in the scale of its transformational drive. If the model repository of images was Venice in the 1960s, and Los Angeles in the 1980s, our imagination today seems to be captured by the barely tethered upheaval of Shanghai. Typology has become associated with a rather well-mannered, even restrained, emphasis upon spatial and temporal continuity – something incompatible with the natural impulses of talented architects eager to explore the formal potentials of the new urban maelstrom. Yet the problems which disabled typological work are separable from its central logic and ambitions, which today appear more legible in Colquhoun than in the Italian rationalists, and in what follows we'll want to contribute to its revitalisation.[3]

Jeffrey Kipnis has remarked that 'diagrams underwrite all typological theories', a comment intended as a link between Durand and Deleuze.[4] Diagrams, as we are thinking about them here, work to constitute and organise decision-making fields, and by this we are not referring simply to making choices among known ends. Instead, diagrams are the collective name given to the patterning of materials and functions that cluster around reasoned reflections in a domain of action and experiment. This makes them especially relevant to urbanism, as a domain in which action places the subject itself in question. Diagrams lend structure and consistency to the ways specific material constellations or media, such as architecture, address a general field of problems, issues and practices, such as those of urbanism. As Stan Allen has pointed out, 'the diagram does not point toward architecture's internal history as a discipline, but rather turns outward, signalling possible relations of matter and information'.[5] Since architecture cannot be simply the tool of any one discursive field – and, correspondingly, neither is the urban governed and instrumentalised through any one technical discipline – architecture's disciplinary density and autonomy serves its ability to respond to complexity and plurality.

But, with what domains of material organisation does architecture respond? One might quickly nominate any among geometry, or form, or structure, and while each of these is necessary to architecture they are each too reductive to clarify how the field engages or enfolds its outside. Architecture responds by understanding, or diagramming, its material resistance to alteration and emergence, its capacity for integrating and organising matters and functions. Inherent in this understanding is a conceptualisation of the relation between repetition and singularity or, if you will, between the elasticity and thresholds of particular material organisations. It is a matter of resolving to think in groups and series while aiming towards material and organisational specificity. This is what typological reasoning in architecture aims to do. These are the broad terms with which Moneo initiated his review of typology, but there are two crucial differences between his account and one which would incorporate diagrammatic thinking into typology. The first is that he gives no attention to the particular way that architecture's outside is converted into graphic form and made available to architecture. As Allen continued while discussing the diagram, 'since nothing can enter architecture without having been first converted into graphic form, the actual mechanism of graphic conversion is fundamental'.[6] Secondly, the underlying tendency of Moneo's essay is to affirm both a continuous history of typology reaching back to Quatremère de Quincy, and to treat the natural schema of this typology as based upon form–content relations. Since these relations are constantly shifting, his history of typology oscillates between an episodic account of different periods and viewpoints on the one hand, and a search for lost foundations on the other. Diagrams work at a level of abstraction that focuses on what we might think of as matter-matter relations, such as integration, organisation and coordination.[7] These have no universal history of the sort Moneo offers, since they have no fundamental taxonomic structure or essential origin for which we might search, nor are they altered by the vagaries of localisable opinion. A diagrammatic

3 Alan Colquhoun, *Essays in Architectural Criticism: Modern Architecture and Historical Change*, MIT Press, 1981. See especially 'The Type and its Transformations', 42–81.
4 Jeffrey Kipnis, 'Re-originating Diagrams', in *Peter Eisenman: Feints*, Skira, 2006, 196.
5 Stan Allen, 'Diagrams Matter', in *ANY 23* (1998), 17.
6 ibid.
7 This more diagrammatic conception of typology in architecture could be thought of as arising out of a linkage between the writings of Stan Allen and Sanford Kwinter. See their essays in *ANY 23*.

approach to type would therefore demand a different kind of history – one we will not be able to develop here – that would reveal a more differentiated and strategic relationship between architecture and urbanism.

So we will want to say that the diagram inheres in typology. But before we do that, we need to clarify a couple of additional points about the ways that architects have written about typology since the 1960s – not to be exhaustive, of course, but to focus our attention on what typological reasoning has been meant to accomplish and how it sets about its work. We might say that typology appeared as a resource – one already residing within the discipline – which could help the field overcome some debilitating gaps and polarisations confronting architectural work. To someone like Rossi, contemporary accounts of urban genesis had surrendered too much to sociological interpretation, with the further implication that the remedies for urban problems would be secured through socio-functional approaches to design.[8] Both the historical interpretation of cities and current design had become brittle and reductive. There seemed to be no sense of disciplinary autonomy that would allow architecture to respond effectively to its primary domain of action, that of the city. The richer field of formal continuity and differentiation that one could observe in the urban past, irreducible to social or functional explanation, was missing from current practice and reasoning. Typology provided one central component of Rossi's efforts to define an independent domain of formal research. Alan Colquhoun brought the question of design method into sharper focus, noting that contemporary doctrine had left design positioned uncomfortably in a gap between 'biotechnical determinism on the one hand and free expression on the other'.[9] Typology delivered a middle ground – as a means of understanding how previous formal solutions encountered the plurality of conditions, as well as a pattern of reasoning for guiding architectural transformation. In both cases, typology was the name given to an effort to understand and systematise a formal and organisational intelligence native to architecture.

In these cases and others, what typology promised was a way to reason about architecture, its structural variations and transformations and its role in urban change – and to do so as a discipline with some effective autonomy. Typology was seen to link current practice to what Eisenman would later call architecture's anteriority; it established a system of description, classification and analysis, and opened up a line of reasoning about formal continuity, organisation and differentiation independently of any simplistic understanding of function. While these may have formed some of the rationale for turning to typology, there was little agreement on exactly how typological reasoning should be pursued. Colquhoun treats it as an ineluctable component of design reasoning, only to leave his readers with the uncomfortable sense that we haven't decided whether typological analysis should be rooted in symbolic or organisational qualities. Both readings are available in his writings and invite further clarification. As a starting point, we might think of this schism less as a theoretical error and more as indicative of a conceptual switch present within the field: modernism had created the possibility for architecture to signify independently of its organisation or content. Again, to take a second case, Moneo's 1978 essay, 'On Typology', slips back and forth between treating it as a mode of formal and organisational reasoning on the one hand, and as a means of defining a determinate relation between architecture and history on the other. As a result we are left uncertain as to whether modernists broke from typology on account of their efforts to discard academic precedent or, rather, redefined the foundations of formal reasoning and in doing so reinvented typology. The point today is not so much to return to these writings to make final decisions on their terrain, but rather to question how this apparently central constellation of disciplinary reasoning should have been so difficult to pin down.

8   Aldo Rossi, *The Architecture of the City*, MIT Press, 1982, first published in 1966.
9   Alan Colquhoun, op. cit., 46.

The first thing to notice about typology is that it is absolutely dependent upon architecture's investment in the two-dimensionality of graphic production. It is via the graphic that critical analysis and design can become linked. This involves both a conversion of the built into drawing and a conceptualisation of how drawing projects another materialisation. To point this out is simply to highlight what has been a central tradition in architectural writing in recent decades, from Colin Rowe through Robin Evans to Stan Allen: the scrutiny of the transactional character of architecture's graphic discipline. Much of the real core of architectural training and production involves moving effectively between the material world of building and inhabitation and the virtual world of graphic exploration. Lately, the increasing interest in the diagram as the conceptual instrument for this movement has initiated a series of more theoretical discussions that have lured architects and historians back to the writings of Charles Sanders Peirce (1839–1914). The aim has been to find in his writings a resource for understanding the ways different sorts of drawings work as particular mechanisms of conversion between the material and the virtual. Since this has all been repeated many times, we won't want to linger on Peirce for long. But there are some interesting points of divergence on the understanding of architectural signs, and more importantly, these discussions shed some light on aspects of those typological writings from the 1960s and 1970s.

We may rely upon Anthony Vidler's recent, concise account of Peirce's theory of signs to explore these issues.[10] To set the stage, all thinking is pursued through signs, and all signs have objects which they represent. Peirce then divides signs into three groups depending upon how they represent their objects, naming the icon, the index and the symbol. All three are said to work by exciting the idea of the object they represent, and so we might imagine an element of interpretation to be always present within the process. If we focus our attention just on the icon and the index, the former works by resembling its object, while the latter works by registering a material force or contact we would take to indicate the presence or action of the object. The usual child's drawings of the house or the flower are simple instances of icons, while the index is often exemplified by a footprint in the sand, a thermometer or a fingerprint on glass. An interesting discrepancy emerges if we compare a brief comment by Vidler on the photograph with a statement by Stan Allen. Vidler allows the photo into the category of icons on account of its work as a likeness of its object, while Allen follows Susan Sontag's initiative and emphasises the materiality of the trace embodied in the photo and consequently considers it as an index. The point of this is not to refine the theory of signs extending back to Peirce, but to notice that graphic signs may contain a kind of tension between indicating their object through likeness or by registering the material forces that drive their formation. To put it differently, architecture – buildings and drawings alike – may be understood and differentiated by what they look like or, alternatively, by how they are made – the patterned material organisations and functions that reside in their formation. The implication is that architecture will always be subject to a kind of interpretive/performative tension and, we might add, for good or ill.

We'll want to bring the discussion back to typology more directly in a moment, but first let's take the matter of signs a step further. Vidler goes on to tell us that Peirce recognised different kinds of icons, and grouped diagrams among those 'that mark out the internal and external relations of their objects in a more abstract way, analogously'.[11] These are particularly useful for thinking because of the way they filter out less important information and focus on key relationships. Peirce was the son of a Harvard professor of mathematics and astronomy, and was himself trained in philosophy and chemistry, so we might understand his keen interest in trying to capture the communicative intersection of general and technical reasoning. Diagrams, he explained, were essential elements in patterns

10 Anthony Vidler, 'What is a Diagram Anyway?'
    in *Peter Eisenman: Feints*, op. cit., 19–27.
11 ibid., 19. See also Stan Allen, 'Trace Elements'
    in Cynthia Davidson (ed.), *Tracing Eisenman*,
    Thames & Hudson, 2006.

of scientific experimentation and discovery because they captured a certain state of dynamic things in such a way that their relationships could be observed. [12] Abstraction was the key to this: the image was not final or complete, but rather one that encouraged the consideration of permutations. Diagrams become particularly useful for projecting a series of possible transformations, testing and clarifying their implications. One shouldn't confuse this with a catalogue of endless possibilities, which one might peruse distractedly. It is more a sequence of potential states that require our reason and attention: one diagram leads to others, as if in a chain reaction, incorporating new elements along the way and forming something like a composite field of linked relationships. Diagrams clarify the kind of thought that would allow one to respond to the outside conditions or premises of the medium one is working with. Vidler tells us that diagrams understood in this way are both the mirror and the instrument of thought – they are graphic indications of a reasoned order occasioned by the intersection of material environments. [13]

The understanding of the specificity of these material environments is quite important for architecture, and in a double sense. Remember that the diagram is characterised by its capacity to register internal and external relationships. This helps to clarify further how a diagrammatic series differs from a catalogue, in that the latter offers a contingent choice among final states such that the external conditions are left pending. Because diagrammatic series reflect our consideration of the way that the specific material of our field will encounter and respond to external conditions, they also become an instrument for diagnosing those conditions. The encounter of two different material domains instigates a kind of projective and interactive testing. Now we can understand why Kipnis would have made that interesting comment in relation to Durand's famous tables: these tables are neither diagrams nor are they properly catalogues, but they indicate how architecture might begin to consider its material organisation so as to become amenable to diagrammatic reasoning. Werner Oechslin made a similar point in his 1986 essay inviting architecture to take up a fresh consideration of typology. [14] For him, Durand's tables show how architecture might begin to order and reason about its material capacities in relation both to its history and to its potential for responding to current conditions with increasing complexity.

What we should notice is that the figures in Durand's tables are icons. However, as Oechslin is suggesting, they also contain that legible tension that inclines one to read them as indexical. How would they be made? What agencies would have been involved in their formation and selection? Now here is what is most interesting: both typology and the diagram depend upon the possibility of this double reading in the abstraction of Durand's signs. This is not to suggest that all typological reasoning depends upon the understanding of architecture registered by Durand in the early nineteenth century. On the contrary, both the abstraction and the organisation would be subject to review, updating and reorientation. Much more still could be said about Peirce and signs, but let's simplify the matter and recognise that what interested Peirce in the differences among icons was that some tended to reinforce the sense of immediate presence between the subject and the likeness of some object (which might be very useful for designation, say), while others tended to specify relational sets (useful for interrogation and experiment). Finally, there is also the index, which encourages us to take note of conditions, forces and agencies that stand behind the formation and selection of architectural material. Architectural drawing inclines toward all three.

When we first mentioned the diagram in relation to Kipnis and Allen and the deficiencies of typological writings, we were discussing it as a conceptual apparatus for linking or constituting relationships between a domain of material practice and its outside. To do this is a matter of enfolding, or 'complicating', the immanent relations within the

12 Vidler, ibid., 20.
13 ibid.
14 Werner Oechslin, 'Premises for the Resumption of the Discussion of Typology', *Assemblage* 1, 1986.
15 My debt for the term 'complicate' is owed to Sanford Kwinter, who was drawing our attention to the older meaning emphasising how folding added complexity and interest to a material surface. See Kwinter op. cit.

discipline or medium so that it can communicate or engage effectively with its outside.[15] The relationship of architecture and urbanism can be described in this way. This version of the diagram is not precisely visible, and so should not be collapsed together with the diagrammatic icons Peirce describes. In fact, this complication of architecture's interior can sometimes be difficult to draw in itself. Students often assume that the bending, bundling or densification of lines suggests complexity, but most architects recognise that in Le Corbusier and Mies alike this would probably just locate the toilets or the kitchen. Instead, the graphic challenge is to clarify how the material of architecture can help us distinguish functional environments from one another in innovative ways – a problem of matter and information. Sanford Kwinter believes this problem might best be explored through cybernetics.[16] He suggests there are three primary phenomena involved in relationships of this sort: integration, organisation and coordination. We might usefully quote him at length regarding the first of these in order to clarify the level of abstraction they describe.

Take the phenomenon of integration: What is it? Where is it located? To explain the problem I will simplify it greatly by limiting it to a figure/ground example. An active ground, one can say, poses a continual threat to the figure upon or within it unless that figure (1) is itself active and flexible, (2) is in continual communication with the ground through feedback loops moving in both directions, and (3) constitutes within itself a system of even greater density of correlations and exchanges so that it can throw up a boundary of order, or a discontinuity between itself and the world that surrounds it. The figure both integrates its surrounding the way a lens focuses and intensifies ambient light, but it also integrates the events in the ambient environment (the changes) which function as a kind of motor for it, a thermodynamic potential to be tapped.[17]

The account can be read at several levels of concreteness or generality, and seems to invite our consideration of both discursive relations and functional/material relations together. This seems to me to describe well the combination of reason and practical knowledge that would become unified in the use of diagrams.

These conceptual diagrams may be difficult to convert to drawing; however, in every medium or domain of material practice, thought searches out means of coordinating functions, of characterising relationships and, in general, of giving density and complexity to the organisation of its elements. From Peirce's perspective, these ambitions lead each field to generate the specific and visible diagrams relevant to its own material domain. So we might associate the diagram as a conceptual apparatus with the myriad instances of graphic diagrams shaping the thoughts of particular disciplines, without wishing to turn them into an identity. If we accept Stan Allen's earlier point that the question of conversion between the material and the drawn is fundamental, we have just learned, nevertheless, that this poses a considerable challenge to any architectural work that aims towards experimentation and complexity.

In a brief and indicative way, we may suggest that the pathway through this challenge leads through type, and to do this we will quickly touch on two important essays in the typological literature. Giulio Carlo Argan's essay of 1963, 'On the Typology of Architecture', indicates some of the conceptual difficulties we encounter with this genre.[18] To begin with, Moneo notes that Argan saw type as 'a kind of abstraction inherent in the use and form of series of buildings'.[19] On first take, this seems encouragingly close to our position, particularly because of Argan's additional reference to Quatremère de Quincy's well-worn distinction between the type and the model. We understand from these points that the type should initiate thought rather than imitation. But the impression of agreement quickly begins to drift and falter. First, Argan clarifies that types can only be deduced from building projects 'a posteriori'. How? Type would emerge through a certain 'comparison and

16 ibid.
17 ibid., 60.
18 Carlo Giulio Argan, 'On the Typology of
    Architecture' in Kate Nesbitt, op. cit. See also
    essays by Moneo and Oechslin, op. cit., for their
    discussions of Argan's essay and its significance.
19 Moneo, op. cit., 36.

overlapping of certain formal regularities'.[20] Obviously, this would tell us little of the kind of abstraction that Kwinter has in mind. In fact, Argan moved in the opposite direction in linking type to iconology. Types, he believed, should be read more in relation to the way they signify their ideal affinity with content, rather than for their reasoned relation to material experimentation. Secondly, as Oechslin later went on to point out, this turns the projective difference between the model and the type into one of simple historical or geographical contingency. Rather than being a discursive reflection on the capacities of architecture, type becomes a mundane catalogue of options in relation to particular conditions.[21] Not surprisingly, for Argan, type would contribute little to either the problem of formal definition or the discipline's experimentation.

For a far more helpful direction, we might turn to Colquhoun's 1972 essay, 'Displacement of Concepts in Le Corbusier', grouped under the heading of 'The Type and its Transformations' in the later compilation of his writings.[22] Here, Colquhoun is at pains to illuminate the distinctiveness of Le Corbusier's graphic understandings, pointing out the persistent sense in which the material tradition of architecture is probed for its potential and transformational elasticity. Graphically, Le Corbusier's work suggests that 'the original practice and the new prescription constitute a paradigmatic or metaphoric set, and that the new can only be fully understood with reference to the old, in absentia'.[23] Colquhoun traces the logic of abstraction at work in the five points, demonstrating how they constitute a kind of diagrammatic reflection on architecture's material. Jeffrey Kipnis recently had this to say regarding the work of diagrams in Le Corbusier: 'the five points collaborate at Savoye to erase the privileged status of the ground that architecture before it so strived to reinforce, transforming it into but one datum among many... It works for me and on me, but I can understand why others just see a nice-looking house.'[24] Kipnis is pointing out the multiple levels of le Corbusier's use of architectural signs: some will see just the icon of the house; others, like Kipnis, will observe the reasoned transformation of the field and its material. In relation to both cases, however, Le Corbusier's architecture is an index of fresh agencies bringing about the transformation of material environments. As Colquhoun describes it, Le Corbusier's work runs through a meticulous use of the architectural icon to designate a material domain of transformation. Given the typological status of Le Corbusier's work and its role in guiding repetition and differentiation, it is worth pointing out that what selects type is not its general meaning or symbolisation, but its capacity to constitute fields of organisational experimentation.

What would occasion or re-initiate typological work in architectural urbanism today? We have rejected the reference both to universal history and the particularity of content. We have rejected an overarching and abstract structural taxonomy and the simplicity of orthogonal geometries on which it could be based. We have rejected continuity with an urban image or other context. Yet the persistence with which typological reasoning makes itself felt in all of the arts and domains of material innovation suggests we continue to experiment and speculate in anticipation of a future resurgence of typological debate in architecture. The idea that the diagram inheres in a dramatically reformulated typology would offer one direction for encouraging that future discussion.

20 ibid.
21 See Oechslin's excellent critique of Argan's essay, op. cit.
22 Colquhoun, op. cit.
23 ibid., 51.
24 Kipnis, op. cit., 194.